Job Interview Questions S

MW00326001

LEADERSHIP

INTERVIEW QUESTIONS
YOU'LL MOST LIKELY BE ASKED

250
Interview Questions

VIBRANT
P U B L I S H E R S

LEADERSHIP
INTERVIEW QUESTIONS
YOU'LL MOST LIKELY BE ASKED

© 2021, By Vibrant Publishers, USA. All rights reserved. No part of this publication may be reproduced or distributed in any form or by any means, or stored in a database or retrieval system, without the prior permission of the publisher.

Paperback ISBN 10 :   1-949395-90-1
Paperback ISBN 13 :   978-1-949395-90-7
Ebook ISBN 10:   1-949395-91-X
Ebook ISBN 13:   978-1-949395-91-4

Library of Congress Control Number: 2020937063

This publication is designed to provide accurate and authoritative information in regard to the subject matter covered. The Author has made every effort in the preparation of this book to ensure the accuracy of the information. However, information in this book is sold without warranty either expressed or implied. The Author or the Publisher will not be liable for any damages caused or alleged to be caused either directly or indirectly by this book.

Vibrant Publishers books are available at special quantity discount for sales promotions, or for use in corporate training programs. For more information please write to **bulkorders@vibrantpublishers.com**

Please email feedback / corrections (technical, grammatical or spelling) to **spellerrors@vibrantpublishers.com**

To access the complete catalogue of Vibrant Publishers, visit **www.vibrantpublishers.com**

Table of Contents

Dear Reader,

Thank you for purchasing **Leadership Interview Questions You'll Most Likely Be Asked.** We are committed to publishing books that are content-rich, concise and approachable enabling more readers to read and make the fullest use of them. We hope this book provides the most enriching learning experience as you prepare for your interview.

Should you have any questions or suggestions, feel free to email us at **reachus@vibrantpublishers.com**

Thanks again for your purchase. Good luck with your interview!

– Vibrant Publishers Team

facebook.com/vibrantpublishers

About the Author

 **Yvonne Marie Valladares** is a Human Resource Consultant and Medical Compliance Manager of A Healthy Mix Management LLC. For 11 years, she has consulted with many start-up companies helping them to build their brand, team and provide continuous employee development. She is a captivating speaker and an unrelenting, often irreverent team builder. She truly believes an organization will succeed if their employees are not only highly qualified but also engaged. Yvonne lives and continues to thrive in New Jersey taking on one start-up at a time.

This page is intentionally left blank

1

Competency

Behavioral

Opinion

Situational

Credential Verification

Experience Verification

Strategic Thinking

Character and Ethics

Management Style

Communication

001. Was there a time where you were called upon to reorganize your department? If so, what steps did you take to ensure the reorganization was successful?

Answer:

The candidate should be able to relate a verifiable time when she was asked to reorganize her department. The correct answer should say something like, "just last year my company decided there should be reorganization program because the internet had significantly changed the way we were doing business."

As an example:

My first step was to identify the exact business functions that were driving the need for change. Secondly, I identified the functions that were working properly and should not be changed. Thirdly, I made a determination of how the people in the department needed to be reassigned to best accomplish the reorganization. In the end, the reorganization was successful, and the company's profits where increased.

002. Please tell me about a time when you led a team to successfully complete a project.

Answer:

The correct answer should describe a real situation in which the candidate led his team to complete a project.

As an example:

Last year my management team was assigned the task of finding a way to improve our company's overall customer service rating. We were having trouble finding and retaining customer service representatives that were responsive to the needs of our customers.

Through customer service surveys and close observation of customer service interactions, we were able to identify several customer service representatives that were providing outstanding service to our customers. We assigned these people as trainers and mentors for the purpose of motivating the entire staff to provide a high level of service to our customers.

003. Please describe the most significant challenge you have faced in a leadership position.

Answer:

The candidate must have leadership experience to answer this question correctly. The interviewer will be able to discern right away if the candidate is trying to bluff his way through the question. The only way to answer the question correctly is to have handled a real situation as a leader.

As an example:

When I was serving as the senior accounting manager at my last employer, we had an incident involving the misappropriation of funds by a member of the accounting staff. This person had been quietly transferring money from the company to a secret checking account for a period of two years. When I discovered the loss, I had to alert both company leadership and law enforcement. I also had to find a way to mitigate the financial harm that had been done to the company. It will take a long time for the legal process to prosecute this man, and a long time before the company recovers the stolen money.

004. How do you think you will be able to help this company produce a product a consumer will buy?

Answer:

This is a question that is best answered by a candidate who has experience in a manufacturing environment. The candidate may have experience in research and development, or in the actual production of manufactured goods. Of course, people who develop software are producing a product for consumers. So, the question has broad application to many industries in which something valuable is being produced.

As an example:

As a member of my last employer's research and development team, I led the process to develop an educational software package that will help kindergarten children to improve their reading speed and comprehension. I will bring this same level of leadership to this company if I am hired for this position.

005. How do you think you will be able to help this company improve customer service?

Answer:

This is a basic leadership question. Many of the jobs in our country are found in the customer service profession. As a customer service leader, the candidate should be able to provide some verifiable evidence that he knows how to lead the company's customer service efforts.

As an example:

I have several years of experience leading customer service departments to meet the needs of customers. In my last job, I was able to lead our customer service department to receive a satisfaction rating of 95%. This was the highest customer service rating the company had received in its 20-year history.

---

006. Are there particular steps that a company should take to develop the leadership skills of its people?

Answer:

I believe there are a number of steps that can be taken. Companies should be interested in the advancement of the qualified people who work for the business.

As an example:

The first step is to identify employees who seem to have a natural affinity for leadership. Additionally, there are probably other people in the company who could be a good leader if they were mentored by someone in the company who had already been proven to be a good leader. Secondly, human resources need to identify educational or training programs the potential leaders could be enrolled in to help them develop their leadership skills. Finally, the best school is experience. The new leaders should be assigned positions that allow them to hone their skills. These steps can be used by any company to help their employees grow professionally.

---

007. Are you satisfied with your personal leadership style and skills? If not, what are your plans to improve your style or skills?

Answer:

When answering this question, the candidate will provide one of two answers. If the candidate is satisfied with his leadership style and skills, he may need to provide a compelling answer that supports that viewpoint. If the candidate is not satisfied with his leadership style and skills, he will need to explain his plans for improvement.

As an example:

I know I need to develop my leadership skills. I have developed a list of books on leadership that I am working my way though. Additionally, I am attending as many seminars on leadership that I can. Finally, every time I make a decision that does not go to well, I search out someone in the office who can provide me some insight as to why I may have made an incorrect decision.

008. Please describe what you think are the proper steps to take when disciplining an employee.

Answer:

Determine the circumstances surrounding the incident, respond patiently, talk to the employee in business-like manner and complete the session.

As an example:

The last time I disciplined an employee I used the steps I just outlined in my initial answer. I think the key to success in the process is ensuring the entire transaction is conducted in a business-like manner. If the counsellor allows the conversation to get overly emotional, the employee will leave the meeting very bitter without encouragement to improve his duty performance.

009. How do you set up priorities for the work you are facing each day?

Answer:

My daily work scheduled must be prioritized so that the most essential responsibilities of the day are taken care of first. Of course, I must respond to any emergencies as they occur. I have learned how to set aside non-essential tasks until a later time. I do not allow non-essential tasks to side track me from the tasks that must be accomplished to keep the business moving forward.

As an example:

Every morning when I come in, I try to determine which tasks or responsibilities must be accomplished to ensure the continued operation of the company. I then make sure I am able to make all of the essential meetings on my schedule. I also must make sure I have time to meet the needs of the people who work in my department. Since good people are the key to any company's success, managers must make sure there is time to respond to their needs.

010. What you do if you became aware that your company's leadership was not enforcing employee safety standards?

Answer:

The candidate should show a proper regard for the enforcement of safety standards in the answer that is provided to the interviewer. This is a serious subject because employees should not fear being harmed at work. The candidate should indicate to the interviewer that he would take action to ensure safety standards were being enforced.

As an example:

If I learned safety standards were not being enforced, the first step is to go approach the person in charge of safety and find out if the accusations are true. Since my job is important to me, I must proceed carefully. If the company will not enforce safety standards, the only option that may be open to me is to file a report with OSHA. I believe that every person in a leadership position must ensure that all workplace safety regulations are enforced.

011. Are you good at delegating responsibility?

Answer:

For most organizations, the answer to this question must be yes. In the modern fast paced business environment, no leader can keep up without the ability to delegate responsibility.

As an example:

When I was hired for my last position, I was overwhelmed by the workload. I soon learned that I couldn't fulfill all the responsibilities by myself. I quickly established a plan to spread my work to others in the division who had the appropriate level of professional responsibility to be trusted with essential duties. Now more work is being accomplished than one person was doing in the past.

012. How do you create an environment of respect within your organization?

Answer:

The correct answer is, "in today's business environment, respect is an essential element of an organization's efforts to treat its customers and employees fairly and justly. The creation of an environment of respect must start at the highest level of the organization. Senior leadership must set an example of respect and must set an expectation that anyone in the organization who cannot show respect to other people will not have a place in the organization."

As an example:

The last company I worked for made sure that respect for other people is part of the company's statement of core values. Senior leadership has made it clear to employees at every level that any disrespectful attitudes or actions will not be tolerated.

013. How do you define personnel management?

Answer:

The correct answer to this question should include a statement such as, "personnel management includes all the actions to recruit, retain, support and make sure an organization's employees are satisfied with their job."

As an example:

When I was an assistant department manager for human resources, I was responsible for keeping the company benefit plan competitive with the other companies that had the capability of luring our best employees away. I spent many hours talking to our people, to company leadership and to the companies that we contracted with for benefits such as health insurance. I had to maintain a system of benefits that were attractive to our people.

014. How do you keep external forces from negatively impacting an organization's core values?

Answer:

A company's core values are principles a company stands for such as honestly, equity and outstanding customer service. External forces such as pressure from competitors can push a company away from its core values.

As an example:

The primary way that a company resists external forces is the commitment of senior company leadership to maintain absolute adherence to its core values. Senior leadership must insist that at no point would the company move away from treating its customer's honestly, fairly and with respect. The pressure to maintain the largest market share cannot be allowed to move a company away from its core values.

015. What evaluation tools do you use to set your personal goals?

Answer:

The evaluation tools I use are designed to help me determine if the decision makes good sense financially, makes good sense professionally and will improve the quality of life my family enjoys.

As an example:

For financial planning, I use the financial planning software that is available on my bank's web page. I don't make a move in any direction unless I am sure to the best of my ability that my family will not be placed in financial jeopardy. The method I use to plan for my professional growth involves talking to and listening to people who have already moved down the path I need to travel to success. Finally, I do not make a move in any direction if I can see that my family's standard of living will be negatively impacted. My wife and I have agreed that I will not make any risky moves unless we are both in 100 per cent agreement.

016. What is your definition of diversity in the workplace?

Answer:

Workplace diversity can mean people with different cultural backgrounds, or it can mean people have many different belief systems, or people can have many different political viewpoints.

As an example:

In my last department, we had people working for us from all over the world. I set the tone by letting everyone in the department know that regardless of where their coworkers came from, I expected everyone to be treated equitably. The diverse cultural background in my department provided us with a rich blend of skills and talents we might have never experienced otherwise.

017. Can you tell me the most important duties of a human resource manager?

Answer:

When answering this question, candidates may provide a wide range of opinions. The company a candidate is applying to will have its own opinion on which of a human resource manager's duty is considered the most important.

As an example:

I feel the most important duty of a human resource manager is the recruitment of high-quality workers. The company's competitive advantage is based on the quality of the people working for the company. If the HR manager is unable to hire high quality people, the company may find itself losing market share.

018. As a fast food restaurant manager, how would you define or describe exceptional service in a fast food restaurant?

Answer:

When answering this question, candidates may provide a wide range of opinions. Each fast food restaurant chain will have its own standards for exceptional service and will examine the candidate based on those standards.

As an example:

As a fast food restaurant manager, I have always expected the customer to be waited on in five seconds after coming to the counter. Exceptional service also includes getting the customer's order correct the first time and includes ensuring the food is hot and fresh.

019. When a customer hits you with several unrelated questions at the same time, how do you sort through all of the questions and solve the issue that is the most important to the customer?

Answer:

First off, you need to shut up and listen to the customer. If you are patient enough to hear everything the customer is complaining about, a common theme will begin to emerge. If you follow the trend of the conversation, you will eventually get down to the truth.

As an example:

I recently had to deal with a customer that had a whole lot of questions related to a product we sold him that was not working correctly. Some of the customer's questions could have been considered very insulting toward me and toward the company. I held my tongue, was as patient as I could be, and listened to everything the man had to say. I found out that a simple part had broken on the product, and I knew we could fix it very easily. In the end, I was able to restore the customer's confidence in our company.

020. Which performance indicators do you use to measure the job performance of customer service representatives?

Answer:

Every company will have its own standards, but the question is asking the candidate to provide his own viewpoint of performance indicators that should be used to measure the performance of customer service representative.

As an example:

The performance standards that I think are important are customer interactions completed per shift, customer service ratings received from satisfaction surveys and performance evaluations provided by supervisors. If the customer service representative receives top ratings in these categories, she will be in line for promotion and raises.

021. What are some formal or scientific methods for measuring customer satisfaction?

Answer:

Some formal methods for measuring customer satisfaction include customer surveys and accounting procedures that measure repeat sales.

As an example:

All of our customers are asked to complete a customer satisfaction survey at the conclusion of every sale, and the conclusion of every call to our customer service office. Secondly, when a sale is made, our accounting system records who made the purchase by a number assigned to each customer. Over the reporting period, we can track exactly how many times a customer purchases a product from our store.

022. Please tell me what the steps are in organizing a sales team.

Answer:

To answer the question correctly, the candidate must detail his specific plan for organizing a sales team and developing a program that will provide continued profitability to the company.

As an example:

The first step in organizing an outstanding sales team is hiring the best qualified staff of salespeople possible. Second, I would initiate an effective training program, and thirdly I would make sure that each salesperson understood the value of the products to be sold. With these steps in place, I should be able to build a sales force that would bring significant profitability to the company.

023. In what ways can rapid growth be harmful to an organization?

Answer:

Rapid growth can stretch an organizations ability to keep up with demand to the point that something in the system breaks. Organizations experiencing rapid growth must put in place the necessary infrastructure to handle the growth.

As an example:

Rapid growth can stretch labor resources to the point that employees become overburdened with work. Rapid growth requires the expenditure of money the company may not have. Rapid growth can cause employees to lose sight of the organization's core values. Rapid growth requires senior leadership to find creative ways to expand an organization's infrastructure, without straining limited resources to the breaking point.

024. Do you understand the responsibilities required of senior corporate leadership under the Sarbanes-Oxley Act of 2002?

Answer:

There are several sections to the SOX act, and it would take a long discussion to cover all of the responsibilities senior corporate leadership has under this law. However, there is one primary reporting responsibility that company leadership must comply with, that is the certification that the annual report represents information that accurately reflects the financial status of the company.

As an example:

Senior leadership of publicly traded companies must certify that to the best of their knowledge, the annual financial statements that are presented to the public and to shareholders are accurate, and that no off the books transactions are being hid from the public. The penalties for knowingly certifying false financial records are very stiff. Publicly traded companies must comply with stringent auditing requirements. The regulations are designed to eliminate the fraud that some corporate leaders have committed.

025. What is your definition of differentiation in the marketplace?

Answer:

Differentiation in the marketplace happens when a company brings a product to the market that has distinguishing features that sets it apart from competitor's products.

As an example:

Lawn mowers seem to be all alike to many people, but if a company could bring a lawn mower to the market that would have self-sharpening blades, that would be a feature that differentiates this product from all others. The company would expect this feature to increase its sales and increase its market share.

026. What is the relationship of differentiation to competitive advantage?

Answer:

Differentiation and competitive advantage are closely related. It is possible to have a competitive advantage without differentiation, but if a product has a feature that differentiates it from all others, the company will expect this feature to drive its competitive advantage to higher levels.

As an example:

A company that has a very good product may have a competitive advantage because its products are price leaders. When the company is able to improve its product's usefulness to the public through a feature no other competitor's product has, the differentiating feature should increase the company's competitive advantage.

027. What benefit does a company's long-term competitive advantage provide to shareholders?

Answer:

Long-term competitive advantage provides shareholders with increased stock value and profitability.

As an example:

As long as a company is able to maintain a greater market share than its competitors, stock values and profitability will grow. If customers decide to turn away from a company, then shareholders dividends will be in danger of decreasing.

028. Please define a SWOT analysis.

Answer:

SWOT stands for strengths, weaknesses, opportunities and threats. A SWOT analysis is a broad-based searching analysis of a company's operations to determine how the company can be better positioned to take advantage of future opportunities.

As an example:

When a company conducts a SWOT analysis, it will find out which of its processes it is very good at, will find out what it is not so good at, will zero in on how it can grasp future opportunities and will identify any dangers the company may face in the future.

029. How do you lead your organization or company to conduct a SWOT analysis?

Answer:

Company leaders will need to gather information from every corner of the company. Information includes financial records, performance records, labor records and customer inputs. The next step is to develop management teams assigned to explore every operation and process the company conducts.

As an example:

The ultimate goal of all these detailed efforts is to find ways to position a company for future growth. A SWOT analysis must be an assessment that probes very deeply into everything the company is doing. Any waste that is exposed must be eliminated as efficiently as possible and any good things the company is doing must be enhanced.

2

Competency

Behavioral

Opinion

Situational

Credential Verification

Experience Verification

Strategic Thinking

Character and Ethics

Management Style

Communication

030. If a group of people in your department were talking about you behind you back, what do you think they would be saying about you?

Answer:

The candidate may be reluctant to venture and answer for this question, nevertheless the interviewer should press for an answer. This question should shed significant light on the candidate's self-image.

As an example:

I have noticed on occasion that my actions cause some interesting conversation throughout my department. It is hard for me to ignore what is being said. Some people say that I cater to the boss's whims to get my name at the top of the promotion list. All I am concerned about is doing the best job that I can. I can't control what other people say about me.

031. Please tell me what you believe are the two most important leadership traits a leader must have. Please explain your answer.

Answer:

The candidate may name vision, innovative spirit, discipline, dependability, empathy or many others. The key to correctly answering the question is how the candidate frames his response.

As an example:

Number one, I think effective leadership requires the leader to have a strong vision and have the ability to get others to share in his vision. Secondly, I believe effective leadership requires discipline. An effective leader has the discipline to come into work each day and follow all the rules, remain productive and set the example for her team.

032. Has there ever been a time when you failed when working in a leadership role? Please explain what happened.

Answer:
Since no one is perfect, candidates should be able to remember an occasion when they failed to accomplish what they set out to do.

As an example:
I can remember an occasion when I had the responsibility to lead a team tasked to find ways to reduce the company workforce without endangering productivity levels. I was unable to develop an effective relationship with the members of the team. Consequently, the team failed to find a workable solution to the workforce reduction requirements. My reputation as a leader was marred because of this failure.

033. In what ways have you demonstrated leadership to the managers in your department or division?

Answer:
The candidate should answer this question by recounting an occasion when she provided guidance to her department managers helping them understand some of the qualities of good leadership.

As an example:
I have always set the example of making sure the people working for me were well taken care of. People need to have the assurance that their employer is treating them with respect and will not cast

them aside when the company is experiencing difficulties in the marketplace. In fact, our company recently experienced a financial downturn, and I found a way to ensure each of the people I am responsible for received at least 25 hours per week of work until the company was able to turn the situation around. Not a single person in any of the departments I am responsible for lost their job.

034. In your career as a leader, which position brought you the least satisfaction?

Answer:

In this question the candidate has the opportunity to share with the interviewer the kind of work that he really does not want to be involved in again.

As an example:

For a short period of time I had to fill the need my former employer had for a person to head up the receiving department. Every day we had several truckloads of supplies that had to be inventoried and inspected. Almost every day, there were shipments that had received serious damage from mishandling and improper packing. It was a very difficult task to file claims on all of the damaged shipments. I do not want to do that type of work again if I can help it.

035. Why are you thinking about leaving your present position?

Answer:

This is a question that may seem very difficult to answer. The candidate may not want to reveal some of her reasons for changing employers. The interviewer is looking for any answer that reveals unresolved issues the candidate has with her previous employer.

As an example:

I am seeking a change in employment because I feel I have progressed as far as I can in my profession at my last job. I need new challenges, and I am looking for a position where there are real chances for advancement to a senior leadership position. I want to make far more money than my presently position provides.

036. As a leader, how do you define success?

Answer:

Success can be measured by a very wide range of indicators. Success can be measured by the level of income a person earns. Success can be measured by being able to maintain your integrity, or success can be measured by the level of service a person renders to his fellow man.

As an example:

In my many years of professional experience, I have been recognized many times for my outstanding performance. I have a high level of confidence that my work in the field of nursing will improve patient care for thousands of patients. That is the best measure of success I can provide.

037. What are some ways a person in a leadership role can control the pressures related to her position?

Answer:

If a hard-working person is not careful, their employer will pile on so much work the pressure can become overwhelming. The interviewer is interested in finding out exactly how the candidate handles this pressure.

As an example:

I have learned to set boundaries in my professional career. I have learned that I can only do so much. It is hard sometimes to say no to someone who I work for, but in the long run it is best for me, the people I work with and for my family. I have also learned that there are times a person needs to ask for help or learn how to delegate responsibility for projects. In this way, I can relieve some of the pressure by allowing other people the opportunity to excel.

038. Do you prefer working by yourself, or are you more comfortable working in a team environment? If you prefer to work alone, how does that affect your ability to share responsibility for a task with the members of a team?

Answer:

This question can be answered a couple of different ways. The candidate may have a preference for working alone, or the candidate may really enjoy working in a team environment. If the candidate would prefer to work alone, the interviewer is interested in knowing how the candidate overcomes his preference to become an effective team leader.

As an example:

I don't know if forced is the correct word, but the essence of my thought is that I have taught myself the necessity for delegating responsibility to other people. I have learned that I cannot do everything by myself. These lessons have made me a better team member, and an even better team leader.

039. How do you feel when you learn you have made a mistake?

Answer:

I do not feel very good about myself since I pride myself on being able to do each task, I am assigned to correctly the first time.

As an example:

Last month I made a comment to a customer that I thought would be humorous, but the customer thought it was rude. Because of my mistake, I lost that customer's business. I lost a good commission, and the company lost a profitable sale. I felt bad for several days after that.

040. As a person in a leadership position, how well do you take instructions you do not like from your supervisor?

Answer:

The answer to this question should show that the candidate is able to handle themselves in a professional and mature manner, even when presented with situations where they are given instructions they do not agree with. The way a candidate handles these types of situations is a good indicator of their level of professionalism and how well they radiate a sense of calm which will resonate throughout the company. Leaders should handle themselves accordingly and know that their subordinates are watching. Good culture starts at the top.

As an example:

There have been a few times in my career when I have been asked to do something, I had a real distaste for. In the early years of my leadership career, I openly baulked at instructions I felt were unacceptable. Now that some years have passed, I have learned to receive unacceptable instructions with a little more patience.

---

041. As a person working in leadership positions, how do you respond when your boss presents your annual performance appraisal to you?

Answer:

I try to listen, try to understand the counsel being provided. When I am presented with information during a performance appraisal that may not be very positive, I do my best to remain positive.

As an example:

My last performance report covered a period of intense upheaval within the company due to the prolonged economic downturn the country is facing. In order to keep my department going, I had to make several unpopular decisions. I believe that some of my decisions were misunderstood, resulting in negative comments being included in the performance report. The only thing I can do is work toward better results in the next reporting period.

---

042. Please provide me with your personal evaluation of your present employer's greatest weakness.

Answer:

To answer this question correctly, the candidate will need to honestly and fairly describe a weakness that actually exists in her present employer's leadership style, or a weakness in the person's approach to running the business.

As an example:

My present employer has a very difficult time admitting when he has made a mistake. It usually requires a serious customer complaint for him to realize that a mistake was made. I used to get so frustrated at this situation. I have tried to talk to him about the situation, but it has done no good up to this point.

043. What steps to you take to keep opinions expressed by other people around you from influencing your ability to make objective judgments and decisions?

Answer:

Objectivity is not always easy. People who are close to you always have opinions they want you to hear and include as a part of your final decision. An objective leader has to weigh all the evidence and make a decision that is best for the company.

As an example:

The first step is to develop a graphic organizer that allows me to place all of the different opinions in the proper relationship to the problem. The next step is to listen to each person's justification for their opinion. Then I go through the graphic organizer and eliminate the options that do not lead directly to a solution to the problem. This procedure allows me to set aside opinions and ideas that would influence me in the wrong direction.

044. Are you able to remain engaged during long meetings when large amounts of dry facts are being presented?

Answer:

This kind of situation is very difficult for many people. I have to admit there have been times that I started dozing off during long meetings. Of course, I have tried caffeine and energy drinks, but the most professional approach is to find ways to remain attentive such as asking questions when appropriate, or actively taking notes.

As an example:

The last time I had to go to a long and dry meeting, I made plans in advance for staying awake. I brought along my iPod so I could actively take notes, and I interrupted the speaker at every appropriate juncture and involved myself in some active interaction with the speaker. The speaker did not mind the interruptions because they served to keep other people in the meeting attentive. I put this plan in action every time I am scheduled to attend long and dry meetings.

045. Have you personally found any value in taking risks in your professional life?

Answer:

Yes, there have been times when I found value in taking risks. Sometimes the only way to accomplish your goals is to take risks. Just make sure the risks you take have a reasonable chance of succeeding.

As an example:

Early in my career an opportunity for advancement suddenly was presented to me when a manager I was working for suddenly quit his job. Although the job had responsibilities, I was not yet fully qualified to handle, I presented the idea to my boss of allowing me to move up into the position. If I failed to handle the increased responsibilities, I would face the chance of losing my job altogether. I did accomplish all the job required and set the foundation for future success with the company.

046. Are you able to take a broad conception and turn it into an actionable plan?

Answer:

An important skill for technicians who are also leaders is the ability to take ideas and turn them into reality. I believe I have gained the skills to make dreams become reality.

As an example:

I worked in the research and development department at my last job. The company I was working for built top of the line recreational vehicles. The most memorable broad concept that senior management came to us with was the inclusion of gas fireplaces in our most expensive model. This concept touched on a full range of disciplines including fuel, carpentry, engineering and interior design. I was able to pull all of the disciplines together and make the conception become a reality.

047. What is the primary lesson you have learned from your failures?

Answer:

The primary lesson that I learned was that I should never give up, regardless of how difficult the task before me.

As an example:

The greatest professional failure I can remember is a time when I was unable to keep an important client from going to another architectural design company. I had been assigned the project to design a very important building for this client. The client kept demanding changes to my design, and I was unable to make all the required changes as fast as the client wanted the job done. Because of my failure to keep up with the client, the company lost a multi-

million-dollar project. The company did not fire me, but I determined right then that I had to get the schooling I needed to improve my design skills. In other words, I did not give up.

3

Competency

Behavioral

Opinion

Situational

Credential Verification

Experience Verification

Strategic Thinking

Character and Ethics

Management Style

Communication

048. How have the people around you responded to your leadership efforts?

Answer:

The expected answer from the candidate is the people he was leading responded very well to his leadership efforts. The candidate should be able to provide solid evidence that people respond to him in a positive manner.

As an example:

For my efforts over the last year to increase my department's sales performance, I received the highest recognition the company provides. The people working in my department responded in an overwhelmingly positive manner to the programs I installed. My department was able to improve sales performance by 15 per cent.

049. Please describe your strengths as a leader.

Answer:

To answer this question correctly, the candidate should be able to describe the elements of his leadership style that makes him a great leader.

As an example:

One of my greatest strengths as a leader is my ability to motivate people to accomplish tasks, they felt were too difficult for them. Recently I worked with a team to overhaul the way we handled incoming shipments. We have many deliveries come in throughout the day, and our efforts to handle the workload were strained to the limit. Working together, we developed a work schedule that maximized the number of people we had available to meet peak workload requirements.

050. Please describe the greatest weakness in your leadership style.

Answer:

The candidate should answer this question in an honest and open manner. It is hard for some people to admit any weakness, making this question a great indicator of the candidate's willingness to be transparent.

As an example:

There are times I am not as observant as I should be. While working on a project earlier this year, I failed to see that an important element of the plan had been done incorrectly. My error caused us to miss an important deadline. I am working very hard to improve my observation skills.

051. Please tell me how you believe the people who work for you would describe your abilities as a leader.

Answer:

I believe the people who are in my department look at me as a gifted leader. I have always been able to develop a very good working relationship with people.

As an example:

At the end of the last sales period, the people in my department threw a barbeque in my honor. The people in my department recognized how my leadership had enabled them to achieve the sales goals that had been set. As far as I know, everyone in the department has a good feeling about my leadership skills.

052. In your opinion, how important are values to the abilities of a leader?

Answer:

The candidate should tell the interviewer values are an essential part of good leadership.

As an example:

I believe that every good leader should have a value system that helps them stay focused on the things that should be important in their work as a leader. An example of this fact came home to me when some people in my department wanted me to bend the rules so they could have more time off than they were allowed. I had to stand firm and enforce the rules. My value system does not allow me to bend the rules unless I am facing an emergency situation.

053. In your opinion, how important are ethics to the ability to be a good leader?

Answer:

The candidate may start with a definition of ethics. Ethics can be defined as the principle's society recognizes as the expected standards of conduct between people or business transactions.

As an example:

My personal ethics will not allow me to do anything that would cheat a customer or provide a product or service that is substandard. I always do my best to ensure the image presented by the company is beyond reproach.

054. In your opinion, how does a department manager display leadership skills?

Answer:

A department manager accomplishes many tasks that fall under the category of leadership including dealing with personnel issues, scheduling issues, production issues and resource management.

As an example:

When I was serving as the production department manager, there were several occasions when we had difficulty keeping all of our production machines running. When the machines were down not only did we have problems meeting production quotas, but I had to decide which employees to let go early each day. These decisions were very unpopular since loss of work time means short paychecks for the affected employees.

055. Please tell me why you feel you are the best person for this position.

Answer:

The question allows the candidate to brag on himself. For the interviewer, the answer to this question provides insight into the attitude of the candidate towards the company and the position.

As an example:

I am the best candidate for this position because I am very dependable, I am able to make important decisions and I have the necessary experience to lead the sales department to improve its performance by 35% in the next six months. If hired, I will be an asset to the company and to its customers.

056. What attributes do you think are most important to a company's success?

Answer:

The candidate may discuss a number of issues including honesty, equity, integrity, commitment to quality, environmental responsibility, social responsibility and vision for the future.

As an example:

I believe a company must uphold the standards of integrity and the responsibility to produce the best quality products possible to remain profitable. The future of any company rests in its ability to understand where the market for its products will be in 5, 10 and 15 years in the future.

057. How do you view the next five years of your professional growth?

Answer:

Five-year goals are usually thought of as short-term goals. These are goals that the candidate would expect to begin working on not long after being hired. The interviewer would expect to sense some excitement on the part of the candidate as he shares the expectation of meeting these short-term goals through the new job.

As an example:

In the next five years I expect that my work will be good enough for the company to increase my annual salary to $48,000. I know this salary expectation will be justified by the quality and quantity of work I will produce.

058. How do you view the next 10 years of your professional growth?

Answer:

The correct answer to this question requires the candidate to think beyond the immediate goals that may be satisfied simply by being hired for the job. This question requires a response provides evidence the candidate is thinking about professional growth in areas such as education or specialized training.

As an example:

In the next 10 years I trust I will be able to earn a PhD in business management. Along with my educational goals, I intend to turn my doctoral thesis into a published book. The work on these goals should increase my opportunities for promotion.

059. Do you think the process of mentoring a person is an important element of that person's professional growth process?

Answer:

The correct answer to this question would be yes, it is very important to help people grow professionally. There is much to learn by helping other people to grow in their profession.

As an example:

I have learned that few people can progress professionally without a little help along the way. The best place a company can look for people to promote is from within its own ranks. When I have helped others, I have really helped myself.

060. Do you have an opinion of why leaders generally display the same type of leadership characteristics?

Answer:

Yes, I do have an opinion on this subject. I believe leaders display the same leadership characteristics because most of them follow the same general training path and are taught by people who generally believe the same things about leadership skills.

As an example:

Businesses have learned over time there are certain things that work in their business processes. Some accepted leadership styles that are used in business today include being authoritative, includes allowing team members to participate, and includes delegating authority to others. Yes, business leadership generally follows one of the accepted leadership styles.

061. Please describe your feelings about consulting with team members before making decisions.

Answer:

My position is that it is important to listen to as many voices as possible before making important decisions.

As an example:

At the beginning of the year, I had to make a decision about the direction of the year's sales campaign. I was having some difficulty trying to decide which direction to take. I sat down with my sales team and asked each member for their ideas. Together we were able to design a sales program that eventually brought the company significant profit.

062. As simply as possible, would you please describe or define how you view the role of a leader?

Answer:

When answering this question, candidate may say something like, "leaders are people who are primarily involved in the process of guiding, influencing or directing people to accomplish a goal or mission."

As an example:

Our company goal is to gain a 25% share of the widget market in the United States. The leadership of our company is actively directing every facet of our business processes in the direction that will allow us to reach that goal.

063. Do you feel your leadership skills came to you through education and experience, or do you consider yourself a natural born leader?

Answer:

This question allows the candidate to take two different approaches when provided an answer. Some may feel they have natural ability, and others may recognize their abilities have only come through hard work and experience.

As an example:

I do not consider myself a natural born leader. I have spent thousands of dollars on college training, and many years of hard work to produce the leadership skills I have. I know there is much more I need to learn. Some people claim to be natural born leaders, but they still have to prove themselves in the daily grind to keep a company profitable.

064. What is your personal definition of the word cooperation?

Answer:

Cooperation is generally defined as a two or more people working together to reach a common goal.

As an example:

On a practical level, cooperation in the business world includes the effort find sufficient common ground to guide and direct a company to fulfill its mission. Cooperative efforts within the business context will usually lead to increased profitability.

065. Without revealing any personal information, please tell me about the person you enjoyed working for above all others.

Answer:

When I was in the Air Force, I had a supervisor in the dock that was one of the best aircraft technicians I have ever known. We got along very well, and I eventually became his assistant.

As an example:

This supervisor knew the technical manuals very well. It seemed like whatever came up; he was able to find the answer. I spent the rest of my military career trying to emulate the work of this man. I do not know where he is today, but I will never forget him. I learned how to be a professional from this man.

066. Without revealing any personal information, please tell me about the person you considered the worst boss to work for.

Answer:

Many years ago, when I was a salesclerk at a local auto parts store, I had a boss that was very hard to work for. This man provided very little training, yet he expected you to figure out on your own how to look up and sell the full range of auto parts. I did not last very long at this job.

As an example:

One day I answered the phone and took a large order from a local coal mine. I really did not understand what the mine office was looking for, so I really messed up the order. The mine was very unhappy, my boss was very unhappy, and this event led to me losing my job. I learned a great deal about dealing with employees from this experience.

067. How many employees do you personally feel comfortable supervising?

Answer:

I can supervise up to 60 people comfortably.

As an example:

Over the years I have worked hard to develop my ability as a manager and supervisor. My greatest satisfaction comes when I am in a position in which I can help people excel in their own jobs. I have learned how to allow the people directly under me help me to carry the workload during periods of high demand and high stress. This is why I can handle the supervision of up to 60 people.

068. Would you please provide your personal definition of authority?

Answer:

The correct answer to this question should include the idea that in a workplace setting those with authority have the right to lead, control and determine how the people working for you conduct their duties.

As an example:

When I had a job supervising a large number of people, I had the authority to determine work schedules, determine who worked at which machine and had the authority to discipline workers who were derelict in the conduct of their duties.

069. What are some responsibilities you have been assigned that were uncomfortable for you?

Answer:

There are many different job responsibilities that may be provided in response to this question. Whatever the answer, it must be something the interviewer is able to determine was not made up but reflects a responsibility the candidate really did not like doing.

As an example:

One responsibility that I have never liked doing is calling people who do not show up for work. Inevitably they will have some fantastic excuse and will want me to cover up for them with the boss. They will want me to say they had a flat tire, or they got seriously ill at the last minute. I am an honest person who prides herself on being to work on time, and I always have to be the bearer of bad news and tell these people they better get into work as fast as they can.

070. What are three things that contributed directly to your success?

Answer:

The candidate is allowed to provide an answer about any three things that have been instrumental in his success in the business world. The important thing is that the interviewer can determine the three things provided are something that actually benefited the candidate's working career.

As an example:

The three things that contributed to my success in the business world are the support of my parents, the fine education I received in college and the mentor I had at my first job. My parents taught me how to work hard and be dependable, my training in a leading business college gave me excellent preparation in accounting and my mentor helped me to learn all the tricks of the trade that I needed to be the best accountant I could possibly be.

071. What is your opinion of employee feedback programs?

Answer:

In this case, the correct answer to this question is that employee feedback programs are an essential element of a company's efforts at understanding employee satisfaction with the direction the company is moving.

As an example:

It is no longer acceptable for companies to make decisions without considering the impact on the workforce. Since quality employees can become the main competitive advantage that a company enjoys, employee feedback programs allow workers to have an active voice in the decisions that affect their lives. Feedback programs are a major factor in maintaining employee satisfaction rating.

072. Do you expect a leader to make the right decision every time?

Answer:

No, I do not. Everybody is human, and people who are busy will make some mistakes along the way.

As an example:

Earlier this year, my present employer decided to change the software that was being used in the payroll department. The IT provider could not make the software work with our company's existing computers, and we went through an entire month with major glitches in our payroll system. Everybody in the company was very happy. This was a leadership decision that was a mistake.

073. Please tell me what you think of your public speaking skills.

Answer:

The candidate can answer that he has good public speaking skills, or he can answer that this is an area needing improvement.

As an example:

Over the last four or five years I have been working hard to improve my public speaking skills. I have taken several classes to improve my public speaking skills. I also take every chance I can find to get up in front of a crowd and speak. My skills have made me a much better communicator in every level of my professional life.

074. How would you evaluate the place you are at in your career? Please use the following scale to make your evaluation; I am just beginning; I am a journeyman; or I am a mature expert.

Answer:

To answer the question correctly, the candidate should use one of the three evaluation standards provided to evaluate her professional growth in her career. The interviewer may expect the candidate to talk a little about why she feels one of the three measures matches her professional growth at the time of the interview.

As an example:

I feel like I am at the journeyman level in my career. I am very confident about my ability to do my job, I am confident I can assume greater responsibility if called upon to do so, but I also know I have much to learn before someone would look at my work and look at my qualifications and say I was a mature expert.

075. If you had the opportunity, what kind of business would you start?

Answer:

If I had the opportunity, I would like to start a little country store in a small town somewhere in Western Colorado.

As an example:

I have always dreamed about owning a little general store in a small town since a vacation we took about 10 years ago. I really liked the small-town atmosphere, and I like the feeling of freedom that would come from being my own boss. It would be wonderful to get up each day and set my own priorities.

076. What is the most important factor to consider when hiring employees?

Answer:

When answering this question, candidates may provide a wide range of opinions. Each candidate will have his or her own opinion of which factors are most important when hiring people. The answer may provide the interviewer with valuable insight on the candidate's viewpoint on what makes himself a good employee.

As an example:

I believe the most important factor to consider when hiring employees is dependability. I believe the best workers are the ones you can depend on under any circumstance. Dependable workers come to work on time every day, dependable workers can be counted on to get their work done on time and dependable workers are loyal to the company. I believe I have all of these characteristics in my life.

077. As a restaurant manager, how would you define or describe exceptional service in a formal restaurant setting?

Answer:

When answering this question, candidates may provide a wide range of opinions. Each candidate will provide his or her own opinion on what kind of service would be considered exceptional.

As an example:

To me, exceptional service means that the customer receives the best possible reception the very instant she enters the restaurant. The customer should receive the best possible food as quickly as possible and the customer should not feel they are being pressured to leave the restaurant before they are ready to go.

078. What do you enjoy most about working with customers?

Answer:

My greatest joy when working with customers is being able to meet their needs without causing them to spend any more money than is absolutely necessary.

As an example:

In my years working as the office manager for a large dental group, I have been faced with finding ways to provide the dental service people need for the lowest possible cost. I recently dealt with a situation in which a small child needed to have some cavities filled, but her parents were financially strapped. I searched through all the resources that were available through the state and had the great joy of helping this child to get the dental help she needed.

079. What is the most important lesson a call center manager needs to learn?

Answer:

The most important lesson a call center manager can learn is that human beings are at both ends of every transaction.

As an example:

The customer service representative is a human being with a whole set of personal priorities that are important to him. The customer also has a set of personal priorities he or she feels must be met. The task of the call center manager is to help each side of every transaction to have his or her priorities met. When the transaction meets the needs of both sides, then productive business can be completed.

080. What are the most important skills a call center leader must possess?

Answer:

A call center supervisor must be calm and confident at all times. Under no circumstance should a call center leader allow the job to cause her to lose her cool. A call center is a noisy and exuberant place to work. Call center leaders must be able to stay above the fray and have the correct answer every time it is needed.

As an example:

I believe a call center leader should always be able to remain calm under pressure. I have seen many stressful customer calls go wrong because the call center rep did not know how to handle the call properly. Projecting a sense of confidence in handling customer complaints and when supporting other call center reps is always important. When a call gets escalated to the lead worker, it is normally because a customer is very upset and demanding answers. The leader should be able to remain calm, listen, be respectful, and be a good role model for the rest of the staff.

081. How do you rate your own qualifications as a call center supervisor or team leader?

Answer:

I believe I am a very good call center supervisor. My job performance ratings have been the highest of any of the supervisors who work for the company.

As an example:

After 15 years of experience of working in call centers, I have just about seen or experienced everything that can happen in a call

*center. I know how to deal with irate customers, and I know how
to motivate customer service representatives. If you hire me, I am
confident I can be a real asset in any call center job you assign me to.*

082. How important do you feel the issue of environmental sensitivity is to business today?

Answer:

In the 21st century, businesses of all sizes have no choice
but to be sensitive to environmental issues. The general
public expects businesses to follow all local, state and federal
environmental laws. Failure to comply with these laws
exposes businesses to serious legal sanctions.

As an example:

*The auto repair business I work for used to just pour used anti-freeze
down the drain, but new laws in our state now prohibit this practice.
The company was forced to lease equipment that fully recycles used
anti-freeze. The company has no choice but to be environmentally
sensitive.*

083. Is there anything about yourself that disappoints you?

Answer:

My only real disappointment in my professional life that I
would like to have a do-over on is my failure to work toward a
PhD earlier in life.

As an example:

*After I finished my MBA, I decided to stay away from schooling for a
while. The delay caused me to miss out on some valuable promotion
opportunities that would have allowed me to provide a much more*

satisfactory standard of living for my family.

084. What is there about you that makes you proud?

Answer:

I am very proud of the time I spent in the Air Force. I received the highest possible recognition for my work in the aircraft maintenance field.

As an example:

I spent most of my Air Force time working on air refueling tankers. Through my efforts to improve a number of maintenance operations, I attained the rank of technical sergeant. I should have stayed in the Air Force on through retirement. I would be fully retired now had I finished a full career in the service.

085. What is your favorite book on leadership?

Answer:

My favourite book is "What the Best CEOs Know: 7 Exceptional Leaders and Their Lessons for Transforming any Business" by Jeffrey Krames.

As an example:

This book has provided me the encouragement I need to accept new business challenges. The seven leaders discussed in the book took a few calculated risks and reaped great financial rewards. I plan to follow the leadership of these corporate leaders to the best of my ability.

086. How do you rate your ability to adapt your leadership style to changing conditions?

Answer:

Sometimes I am able to adapt to changes, and sometimes change is hard for me. I know I need to work on my ability to adapt to change because advancing technology is changing the workplace almost every month.

As an example:

I have found in recent years that about the time we learn a new process brought on by new technology, some new development becomes available that changes the way we have been doing things. An example is the new card readers that can be attached to cell phones. These new devices provide our sales staff with the ability to make a credit card sale anywhere in the country. This change has caused us to make adjustments to our processes in the accounting department. Leaders must be able to adapt to change to remain relevant.

This page is intentionally left blank

4

Competency

Behavioral

Opinion

Situational

Credential Verification

Experience Verification

Strategic Thinking

Character and Ethics

Management Style

Communication

087. Please describe a situation when you needed to build support within your department for an idea you thought would greatly benefit your company.

Answer:

To answer this question correctly, the candidate should describe a situation which required him to build support for his vision and make his ideas become a reality.

As an example:

I had the great idea of finding a way to get the company to develop a childcare center in our building. It would be very convenient for people with small children who worked the building. The initial start-up costs would be significant, but the long-term benefits in increased productivity would pay for the project. It took me almost two years to make my idea become a reality, but everyone in the company is very happy the childcare center is in operation.

088. During a period of difficult challenges, how did you keep the people working under your leadership motivated and working at the highest possible level?

Answer:

To answer this question correctly, the candidate should be able to describe a time when he provided the motivation necessary to keep all of his workers happy and willing to continue working hard, even if the challenges seemed insurmountable.

As an example:

Earlier this year we were presented with the challenge to increase our production by 25% so the company could meet increased customer demand. At the same time, we received several shipments of raw materials that were of substandard quality. Since the company prides itself of the quality of the product it sells to consumers, we the impossible task of meeting production quotas with very limited supplies of suitable raw materials. I had to work very hard with the people in the receiving department to find enough quality raw materials to keep the production lines running at 100%. In the end, the quotas were met, and everyone was very satisfied with the work we did.

089. If hired to work for this company, how can we best utilize your leadership skills?

Answer:

To answer this question correctly, the candidate should be able to describe or define all of the leadership skills she possesses that apply directly to the job being applied for. Leadership skills may be defined by any using any of the following phrases: having a vision, motivational skill, consensus building, being able to inspire people, being persuasive, developing relationships, leading teams, empathy and having good listening skills.

As an example:

I believe that if you hire me for this job, I will be able to use my leadership skills to increase the company's sales of widgets by 25% over the next year. I have always been able to build a consensus among the members of my department about what needs to be done to meet sales goals. If I am hired, I will be an asset to the company.

090. Please describe your ideas about the need to reward team members for outstanding performance.

Answer:

To answer this question correctly, the candidate will need to provide support for the principle that businesses should have a program for recognizing the outstanding work of its employees.

As an example:

Several years ago, I led a team that proposed a recognition program for company employees. Although all of my ideas were not accepted, I was able to get a program started that provided cash bonuses to employees who presented ideas that saved the company money, or increased company profitability.

091. Do you have enough flexibility in your leadership style to adjust quickly to fast moving events or situations?

Answer:

The one major constant in today's business environment is change. Leaders at all levels must be able to adjust to rapidly changing conditions.

As an example:

At my previous employer I was responsible for the customer service department. We found that customers expected to have the most advanced customer service capabilities on our company web site. I found myself adjusting to new business process on a monthly basis. The only way I could be successful as the department manager was to adjust my leadership style to meet changing business conditions.

092. How effective are you at meeting critical deadlines?

Answer:

The ability to meet deadlines is an essential qualification for leadership. I have always worked really hard to ensure my work was accomplished on time.

As an example:

Deadlines are the life of a newspaper managing editor. Every element of the paper must be ready to go by the same time each day. If some important article or report is late the entire paper will be held up. I have not missed a critical deadline in the last 12 months. I am very efficient at meeting deadlines.

093. Is there a major decision you made that you had to change after more facts came to light?

Answer:

Yes, a decision I made about one year ago had to be changed after I learned that some of the events, I was depending on to support my decision never were really going to happen.

As an example:

Last year the company's accounting department provided me with a financial forecast for the next year that showed we were expecting a 25% increase in revenues from an established product line. Based on this forecast, I increased the workforce in our production facility so we would be ready to meet the increased demand. Three months later, an audit of the numbers the forecast was based upon revealed a serious accounting error. I was forced to lay off all of the extra people that had been hired. This was not a very comfortable decision for me to make.

094. If you had to change a major decision at a later date because you realized you made a mistake, how did the people working for you respond to the change?

Answer:

In the first place, many people do not like a change in their working situation. So, if you make a decision that causes change, and then you have to retract the decision and cause more change, people are not going to be happy.

As an example:

The company I was working for asked to look into options for changing employee time accounting from manual timecards to a computerized system. My team found a software package we thought would work very well for our company's needs. After significant expense and inconvenience to our employees the new system was installed. After just a couple of months we found the new system very difficult to work with for both our accounting department, and for our employees. I had to rapidly switch time accounting back to the manual system and continue the search for a better electronic system. The employees and my supervisors were very unhappy with me for all of the confusion that has been created.

095. If you were a restaurant manager, and a guest found a hair or some other foreign object in his food, how would you respond?

Answer:

To answer this question correctly, the candidate should tell the interviewer that she would immediately respond to the customer's problem. The food would be replaced as quickly as possible, and she would provide the customer with a voucher for another meal. Additionally, the manager should go back into the kitchen and find out who was responsible for preparing this meal, and ensure the necessary training is provided to avert future episodes of this type.

As an example:

About two months ago, I was working as the evening manager at the restaurant. Early in the evening, I was made aware that a customer was very angry about what he perceived to be a hair in his potatoes. Although I did not immediately see the hair when I looked at the food, I went ahead and had the kitchen prepare this man a new dish of his choosing. When the customer prepared to leave, we did not charge him for the meal, and we provided him a voucher for a future visit. The next day we had a training session for everyone who worked in the kitchen. We reiterated the need to secure all loose hair with hats and hair pins. We did not want a reoccurrence of hair in a customer's food.

096. How would you respond to a complaint from a very angry customer?

Answer:

The candidate should indicate in his answer that she would display patience, maturity and empathy for the customer's concern. The candidate should indicate she would do everything possible to respond quickly to the customer's concern.

As an example:

Last month I had to deal with a customer who was very angry about a defective lawn mower he purchased from our store. When I looked at the lawn mower, it was obvious that it had been used to cut some very heavy grass and weeds. Even when the man shouted at me, I remained calm and tried to show a real interest in his problem. The customer did not want to hear anything about his use of the mower to cut materials that were beyond the ability of the equipment he had purchased. I agreed to replace the mower but cautioned the man to take more care if he was going to try and mow heavy weeds and grass with this mower. After the man calmed down, he agreed to use more care with the mower we gave him.

097. How do you respond when your subordinates come to you with personal problems?

Answer:

To answer this question correctly, the candidate must express a valid approach to dealing with personal problems in the workplace. Personal issues that happen off duty are outside of a supervisor's authority unless the problem carries over into the employee's duty performance.

As an example:

Some problems may be simple to address, and others may require a referral to a professional trained to deal with serious personal issues. If a subordinate came to me with a problem my first responsibility would be to be a good listener. If the problem was something, I could handle with a phone call or a simple discussion with the people involved in the situation, I would take the necessary actions to help solve the problem. If the person expressed a serious personal problem I was not qualified to handle, I would begin the process of finding a professional who could discreetly provide the necessary help.

098. How do you keep your supervisors from taking advantage of you?

Answer:

People who are good workers many times find themselves overloaded with work because the boss figures out quickly who he can trust to get the work accomplished. I these cases, workers can find themselves overwhelmed by supervisors who take advantage of the situation. In order to avoid this problem, you need to be firm and tell your supervisor there is a limit to what you can accomplish each day.

As an example:

In a previous job, my supervisor figured out that I could be depended upon to get all of my work done on time and done correctly the first time. As time progressed, my supervisor piled more and more work upon me to the point that the stress began to negatively affect my health. When I became very ill, the doctor told me I had to get out from under the stress or I would seriously jeopardize my health. Through this experience I learned firsthand there is only so much a person can do each day. I no longer allow myself to be taken advantage of in this manner anymore.

099. Have you ever reported directly to the most senior levels of company leadership?

Answer:

Yes, I have; in my last job my worked directly for the Chief Executive Officer of the corporation.

As an example:

In my capacity as the senior sales manager, I worked directly under the Chief Executive Officer. I had direct contact with this man almost every day. Although he allowed me significant latitude in the conduct of my job, he wanted to be constantly updated on the company's sales performance throughout the world. I was able to develop good rapport with this man, and we enjoyed a working relationship that was very beneficial to the company.

100. Was there ever a time you had strong competition for your job?

Answer:

It is possible to say that every person has experienced competition for a job or position at some point in the working career. To answer the question correctly, the candidate should tell the interviewer of a time when he had to work really hard to keep his job or had to work really hard to get a job, he wanted really bad.

As an example:

When I first started working for XYZ Corporation, I began working as a customer service representative. As I looked around at what everyone else in the office was doing, I decided I wanted to be the office manager someday. When I started working towards that goal, I learned there was another woman who also wanted the job. This competition made me work real hard. My hard work paid off, and two years later I got the job I wanted.

101. How have you supported the effort to build respect for other employee's opinions within the organization?

Answer:

Yes, I have been involved in many efforts to build and maintain respect for the different opinions that are expressed by members of the organization I work for.

As an example:

In my experience, there are times when a team has been tasked to develop a program and minority voices are pushed to the side regardless of the value of what the person has to say. When a divergent viewpoint is pushed aside without a fair hearing, I always speak up and demand that every opinion is heard. I believe that every person in the organization has the right of a fair hearing for the opinions he has to express.

102. What would you do if you knew the company you were working for was regularly providing an inferior product to customers?

Answer:

Since I am someone who in only interested in working for a company that is providing the highest quality product to customers, I would be very uncomfortable with this situation.

As an example:

If I was in a position to influence the process, I would begin working within the framework of the company to change the culture and bring the necessary change to provide high quality products to customers. If I was not in a position to influence the process, I might begin looking for a job with a company that was providing good value to consumers.

103. What have you done lately to improve the stability of the company you work for?

Answer:

There are many different ways this question can be answered. The interviewer will be looking for a response that shows actions the candidate completed that made the company he was working for more stable. Reasons for increased stability may include item such as increased profitability, increased market share or increased stability in the work force.

As an example:

One of the things my previous employer needed to increase the chances for long term company stability was increased market share of the worldwide widget trade. Over several months of research and development, I discovered a way to produce a quality product at a much lower cost. We improved the process by finding a supplier that would sell us steel for a much lower rate. The lower cost of production allowed us to sell our product 25 percent cheaper than anyone else in the world, thus increasing our market share by 50 percent.

104. Please describe a time when you had to work with a diverse group of people.

Answer:

The interviewer will be expecting the job candidate to describe and actual workplace situation in which the candidate worked with people having diverse backgrounds.

As an example:

When I was promoted to my first supervisory position in the Air Force, I had a man working for me who was a Sioux Indian. His name was Sgt. Talks Different. This man's greatest dream was to become a real medicine man. He would sing traditional Indian chants while he was working. I learned a lot about getting along with people of far different backgrounds during this experience. (Note to editor, this is a scenario that really happened)

105. Have there been situations when you have experienced difficulty working with a diverse group of people?

Answer:

Yes, when I was a GED Instructor for a local community college.

As an example:

The program I was teaching for was serving people who were receiving state and federal aid and were required to go to school to get their GED. Some of the students were actively involved in gang activity. Over the period of time I worked in this program, we had several serious altercations in the classroom. One day the school actually had to have campus security follow me to my car after to insure I got off the campus safely. This experience was a real eye opener.

106. As a service manager, how would you define or describe exceptional service in an auto repair shop setting?

Answer:

When answering this question, candidates may provide a wide range of opinions. Since the auto repair business is so competitive, individual service manager candidates should be able to voice strong opinions about exceptional service because they are generally the first person to great customers and have the first sales opportunity when dealing with customers.

As an example:

My number one concern when providing exceptional customer service is being able to instill in the customer confidence that our technicians will fix their car correctly the first time, and that we will not try and sell them a service item they do not really need. I want customers to feel like our shop is the best place for them to bring their car for repair year after year.

107. As a department store manager, how would you define or describe exceptional service in a department store setting?

Answer:

When answering this question, candidates may provide a wide range of opinions. The opinions may range from the general "making sure the customer is always taken care of" or "making sure the store is always clean and organized" however, the answer should convey that the candidate understands the concept of good service lies in making sure that the customers are taken care of while also making sure that services delivered are within company policy.

As an example:

As a store manager, my number one goal is to ensure we do everything possible to meet all customer demands. We need to have clerks throughout the store ready to respond to customer requests for help. If we do not have what the customer needs on hand, we will always do our best to order what the customer needs. In a department store it is always best to smile and greet visitors, and project a neat and tidy image for the customer so their shopping experience is a positive one.

108. As a college financial aid department manager, how would you define or describe exceptional service when provided by a college financial aid office?

Answer:

When answering this question, candidates may provide a wide range of opinions. Financial aid offices must help students get the financial aid they need to get into school and have the money to stay in school.

As an example:

When I was in charge of the financial aid office at a local college, I was committed to ensuring no student was turned away from school for a lack of money. We worked really hard to ensure students could pursue their dreams without undue worry about the cost of their education. The value of a completed education was far greater than the actual financial cost it took to get the education.

109. Over the next few years, what do you feel are some of the most difficult challenges that people working in customer service are going to face?

Answer:

I feel like the most difficult challenge that customer service people are going to face in the future is the advances in technology that allows customers to demand greater access to a wider range of businesses committed to supplying the products they are looking for.

As an example:

The company I used to work for was in the business of supplying software to local companies. Since we were located in a remote area of the state, everyone had to come to us for the software they needed.

With the rapid advance in computer and internet technology, businesses in our area are able to order the products they need from other areas. The one primary advantage we had was the excellent service our customer service agents are able to provide. Personal service can be a competitive advantage.

110. How many customer interactions on average do you expect a customer service representative to deal with in a normal eight-hour shift?

Answer:

Depending on the type of business, there will be different standards for customer service representatives. The candidate will present an answer based on his or her own working experience.

As an example:

I believe customer service representatives should be able to handle a minimum of 32 customer service interactions in a typical eight-hour shift. This standard allows for 15 minutes per interaction. If the customer service representative is able to produce a higher number per shift, she will gain recognition as an outstanding customer service representative.

111. Please tell me how you would handle customers who use inappropriate or abusive language on the phone, or face-to-face.

Answer:

This can be a real serious problem for many customer service representatives. The first step is to ratchet down the rhetoric. After the customer calms down a little bit, reason usually returns to the conversation, and the inappropriate language goes away.

As an example:

A customer recently called our office, and he was very mad. This customer was using very offensive language, and our customer service representative was shaken. I took over the situation, and let the customer know he needed to calm down and think about what he was saying before we went any further with the conversation. I informed the man that we would take care of his issue. After some conversation along this line, the bad language stopped, and we were able to solve the problem to the satisfaction of the customer.

112. What will be the most significant issue call centers will need to address in the 21st century?

Answer:

The most significant issue that will need to be addressed is the relationship between technology and the need to foster the human element in every business transaction.

As an example:

Many customers are offended when they make a phone call and all they get is a machine. Many companies have restrictive gateways that customers must go through before they reach a human being. I believe we will need to make sure that allowance is made for people who want to reach a human being, and allowance must be made for people who prefer to use electronic technology to contact a company.

113. When you are directly selling to customers, how important is it to sell yourself, or sell the value of the company you represent?

Answer:

It is essential to sell myself. The customer must have confidence I will not cheat him, and I will provide him with the best possible service. Additionally, I am in the business of selling the value of the company I work for.

As an example:

I recently had a customer who was very hard to work with. This customer considered most businesspeople to be very dishonest. I spent extra time with this customer in an effort to gain his trust. It was a challenging task, but in the end, I believe I convinced this man that I would give him good value for his money and proved to him the company would stand behind the products is sells.

114. How responsive should organizations be to the idea of social responsibility?

Answer:

Every non-profit organization, business and government agency must embrace the idea of social responsibility. Society expects every organization to find ways to have a positive impact on the local community.

As an example:

My last employer assigned four of the assistant managers to form a team dedicated to find ways to be a blessing to children in the local children's hospital. We decided to purchase toys with the money the company had set aside for this project. Our plan included giving age appropriate toys to each child in the hospital. I know our work is and will continue to be a great blessing to the children and their families.

115. As you think back to your last employer, what differentiated your company from your competitors?

Answer:

At my previous employer, I worked as an internet banker. Our differentiating feature was that when people called our customer service department, they always were connected to a real human being immediately.

As an example:

Most of our competitors made people go through a complex gateway of questions before they were able to talk to a human being. Not so at our bank. When you call our customer service, you are immediately connected to a person who is willing and ready to meet as many of you needs as possible. This feature sets us apart from our competitors.

116. What part do company's employees play in setting a company apart from its competitors?

Answer:

Quality employees are the key to any businesses' success. Having the most qualified employees in the business definitely gives your company an advantage that others may not be able to match.

As an example:

My last employer was a very large grocery store chain. There are many competitors in the grocery business all across the nation. Grocery prices do not vary too greatly from brand to brand, but our difference was our people. Customer survey after survey showed us that one of the primary reasons people keep coming back to our stores is the outstanding customer service our people provide. Yes, quality people do make a big difference.

5

Competency

Behavioral

Opinion

Situational

Credential Verification

Experience Verification

Strategic Thinking

Character and Ethics

Management Style

Communication

117. Did you have any leadership roles while you were in college? If so, please describe your roles and how they helped you to develop your leadership style.

Answer:

The best way to answer this question is to say yes, I had some very important leadership roles while I was in college.

As an example:

I was elected the senior class treasurer. We did not have a significant amount of money in the treasury, so it was very important for me to ensure the money was managed in a way that allowed the class to accomplish all of its goals. I learned the value of integrity during the time I served as treasurer. This is a lesson that has helped me all through my career.

118. Please summarize the leadership experience you have that will best benefit this company.

Answer:

To answer this question, the candidate should be able to share information on his experience he had for the last five to 10 years that would be of benefit to this new employer.

As an example:

For the last 10 years I have been the service manager for the local Cadillac dealer. I have been responsible for a shop of 20 mechanics and 6 service writers. The shop has typically grossed over one million dollars a year. The shop was recently recognized General Motors as having the best customer service rating in the entire Northern United States. I will bring this level of leadership experience to bear on the needs of this company if hired for this position.

119. Please describe your responsibilities at your last employer.

Answer:

When answering this question, the candidate will be expected to provide an accurate accounting of her responsibilities at her previous employer. A made-up or inaccurate accounting of the candidate's experience may be a disqualifying answer.

As an example:

I had many very important responsibilities at my last employer. I was directly responsible for the weekly report that senior management used to measure the progress of the company the previous week. My team worked diligently to prepare a report that would provide the information senior leadership needed to effectively control the company's business functions. This information is verifiable through the references I have provided.

120. Throughout your career, have you always been an effective leader?

Answer:

I will have to admit there have been times in my professional career when I have been ineffective in my leadership roles. I have made some mistakes that kept me from being promoted to positions that I really desired.

As an example:

At a previous employer, I was assigned to serve as a regional assistant manager. The most challenging responsibility I had was coordinating all of the training resources across the region. I was unable to keep track of all the training coordinators, which led to many employees being unable to get the training they needed. The consequence of my failures was that I was passed over for promotion.

121. Since you consider yourself a talented leader, what has your present or previous employer offered you to keep you from leaving?

Answer:

With this question, the interviewer is trying to find out some detailed information about what it will take to keep this employee happy if she is hired. If the candidate provides an answer that shows she is asking for more than this company can offer, there may be no reason to pursue this person any further.

As an example:

Over the years I have been able to increase my skill, talent and ability as a professional manager. I have earned an MBA from a prestigious university, and I am at the point that I believe I should be able to move up into a position that can enable me to live a better standard of living. My present employer offered to increase my annual salary to $60,000 per year, along with a premier health insurance package. I turned this package down because I believe I can find a position that will offer me an even greater annual salary.

122. Have you ever had to deal with a situation in which a person working for you had an open disagreement with your supervisor?

Answer:

There are two initial answers to this question. If the candidate has not had a person working for him with an open disagreement with a supervisor, the interviewer may decide to ask the candidate to give an answer to this question based on how he thinks he would respond to such an issue. If the candidate has actual experience in this type of problem, the interviewer will expect the candidate to share how he handled the situation.

As an example:

Earlier this year there was an issue I had to deal with concerning an open argument one of my subordinates was having with my supervisor. The argument revolved around the division of a sales commission between my subordinate and another salesperson. I didn't have any direct control over the disbursement of the commission, but the open argument threatened to cause serious trouble in my department. I was forced to jeopardize my own position when I demanded that all the parties to the argument sit down and work out an agreement that would make each party happy.

123. If you are in a position that requires you to hire people, have the people you hired done well in their jobs.

Answer:

This question would only be asked of candidates seeking leadership positions with hiring and firing authority. The candidate should be prepared to provide the interviewer with verifiable evidence that he hired employees that prospered. If the employees he hired have not done well, the interviewer will be looking for an assessment of why the people he hired were not successful.

As an example:

I have enjoyed the authority to hire people for the quality assurance division. One of the most outstanding new hires was a woman we brought on to keep our inspection records in order. Through her efforts, the quality assurance performance statistics improved by 25 percent. Over the years there have been some new hires that did not work out very well, but overall, I believe I have been very successful picking the right people for our company.

124. What procedures or steps have you implemented at previous employers to improve productivity in your department or division?

Answer:

This question would be asked of a candidate applying for a job in which their skills in production management would be useful. To answer the question correctly, the candidate should provide concrete examples of steps or methods he used to improve productivity or profitability of the company he worked for.

As an example:

When I was hired by my previous employer, I was given the task of finding the areas in our shipping department that were slowing down the processing and shipping of products that customers had ordered. I found that may tasks were being duplicated, causing the process to bog down. The delays were negatively affecting customer satisfaction ratings. I installed a number of new procedures that clearly identified lines of responsibility, so one person was not getting involved in another person's work unnecessarily. My efforts improved shipping department efficiency by 90 percent.

125. How many years of supervisory experience do you have? Please tell me some of the job titles you have held as a supervisor.

Answer:

I have 10 years of supervisory experience.

As an example:

Some of my job titles include team leader, floor supervisor, department manager and senior account executive. I was able to move up to the senior account executive position because of my hard work at identifying improved methods for reaching new customers. After the improvements I suggested were installed throughout the company, profitability increased by 25 percent.

126. At what point in your career did you realize your most enjoyable job would be found in a leadership position?

Answer:
After I had been working in retail about 5 years, I determined that I wanted to be more than just a salesclerk. I realized the perks and benefits I wanted for my life could only be found in management.

As an example:
I began working as a salesclerk in a large department store right after I graduated from high school. As I worked day-by-day, I soon realized that I possess the ability to be a manager, and I wanted to make far more money than a part-time salesclerk was making. I went to school and took advantage of every advancement opportunity the company I was working for offered. I am now a very qualified retail manager and hope to become a regional manager in the not too distant future.

127. How effective are you at evaluating technical data? Please use the following scale as a basis for your answer: novice, semi-skilled, skilled or expert.

Answer:
This question would be asked of leaders in technical fields such as computer or car repair. The candidate's choice would direct the interviewer's further questioning of the candidate.

As an example:

I consider myself skilled IT professional. I have become a very proficient IT technician and team leader. Up to 90 percent of the time I am able to make or direct computer repairs to be accomplished in the expected time frame.

---

128. Please tell me which software applications you can operate proficiently.

Answer:

I am proficient in all the Microsoft Office Suite applications, quick books, internet applications and most proprietary software applications.

As an example:

I have 10 years' experience using the Microsoft Office Suite programs, and the others I indicated on my application. My last job required me to use these programs on a daily basis. I am prepared to be tested on my ability if necessary.

---

129. As a customer service manager, what types of products or services have you worked with?

Answer:

I have worked for large department stores, and I have worked for companies providing mobile telephone services.

As an example:

The most enjoyable job I had as a customer service manager for the cell phone company. I was able to help people get a service they really had a need for. Yes, there were many problems, but I was able to work through all of the problems and provide the highest level of customer service. In many cases, it was simply a matter of making sure all of the technology was working correctly. As a result, the store I worked for had the highest customer service rating in the region.

130. Can you describe some changes you have initiated that improve the way customer service representative communicate with customers?

Answer:

Yes, I can, I helped our company to develop an integrated system that provides excellent telephone communications, provides a customer chat system and provides a completely interactive e-mail communication system.

As an example:

With the increase in computer technology our customers were demanding to be able to communicate with the company 24/7. I was assigned to work with a team responsible for solving the problem. I led the team in the effort to propose to the company that we purchase, install and developed the most advanced customer service system available on the market. The new system has increased our customer satisfaction rates significantly.

This page is intentionally left blank

6

Competency

Behavioral

Opinion

Situational

Credential Verification

Experience Verification

Strategic Thinking

Character and Ethics

Management Style

Communication

131. Please describe a time when you played a major leadership role in a special event.

Answer:

To answer this question correctly, the candidate should be able to describe an actual event in which she was the primary leader. The special event could be a job fair, awards banquet, marketing meeting or other event.

As an example:

Our company is constantly looking for talented people. We feel the greatest competitive advantage we have is our people. In April last year, I was given the responsibility to set up a regional job fair designed to attract college graduates. The job fair was a total success. We had over 1000 recent college graduates come to the job fair. Our human resources people were able to fill all our open positions.

132. Please describe a difficult project that required you to build consensus on a divisive issue.

Answer:

Some candidates may consider this a difficult question to answer. Although it is difficult, the interviewer is looking for the candidate to reveal how he deals with divisiveness in the workplace.

As an example:

We had a project to complete that was so large it required the work of three departments. Right in the middle of the project, a serious dispute arose over which department would take the lead position on the project. Tempers became very hot because of the political infighting. Through many hours of painstaking negotiation, I helped everyone involved find a way to put their best foot forward and receive the recognition they were looking for.

133. Please describe a project or task that required you to develop agreement or cooperation between departments.

Answer:

The candidate should be able to provide tangible evidence that she is able to work with other leaders to get important work accomplished.

As an example:

We had a project to improve the wheel bearings on the tricycles our company sells. My department was in charge of the bearings, and another department was in charge of developing the new wheels that would be used on the tricycle. It took significant interdepartmental cooperation to get the bearings and wheels to the correct size for each model of tricycle the company sold.

134. Please describe a time when you were called upon to demonstrate your leadership ability during an emergency situation.

Answer:

The correct answer should include a verifiable incident when the candidate took the leadership during and emergency situation. The incident the candidate discusses doesn't have to be something that happened on the job.

As an example:

I was on the way home from work when I came upon a terrible automobile accident. People were running around hysterically trying to give the victims aid, but not really knowing what needed to be done. I had some triage training while I was in the military, so I took charge until emergency medical personnel could arrive. I was able to provide sufficient first aid so that the victims survived.

---

135. Can you think of a time when your team was assigned the responsibility to complete a very difficult project? If so, how were you able to solicit a commitment from the team to work at their highest level until the project was fully completed?

Answer:

To answer this question correctly, the candidate must be able to recount an occasion when she was able to lead the people under her direction to meet a workplace challenge that few people would have believed could have been accomplished with the resources available at the time.

As an example:

During the first quarter of the year, a trucking company we depended on for 50% of our shipping from the distribution center to our retail outlets suddenly applied for bankruptcy. We had no warning this was going to happen. My team was immediately called upon to get our logistics system back up and running. Under my leadership, my team found several other trucking companies that had the capacity to immediately respond to our need, enabling our company to meet all of our customer demands.

---

136. In your career as a leader, which position provided you with the greatest satisfaction?

Answer:

This question allows the candidate to share a work experience that was very satisfying, thus providing the interviewer with insight into the kinds of work that may best fit the candidate's qualifications.

As an example:

The job that I received the greatest satisfaction from was when I worked as the manager of the shipping department. Every day was very fast paced, and we were in a position to make many people happy. We satisfied the needs of the different departments to get the products shipped so they could have a return on the money the company had in producing the product, and we made the customers happy by getting the finished products to them just as quickly as possible. I like fast paced work environments.

137. What are some ways a person in a leadership role can relieve the stress he experiences?

Answer:

The interviewer is expecting the candidate to provide some methods he employs to relieve the stress that builds up from making decisions and leading people.

As an example:

In my work as a department manager, stress can build up and become overwhelming. I find that when my stress levels get too high, I become very impatient with the people who work for me. Thankfully, the company has an exercise room that I can visit and relieve my stress. It takes just a few minutes on the exercise bike, and I begin to calm down. I have never allowed stress to build up to a point that I lashed out at the people I work with.

138. Have you ever had the opportunity to serve as a mentor for a young person? If you have served as a mentor for a young person, please describe your feelings about this experience.

Answer:

If the candidate indicates that she has served as a mentor for a young person, then the interviewer will expect the requested description of the experience. It is not a wrong answer if the candidate never served in this capacity.

As an example:

In my local church I volunteer in the teen department. There was a young man coming to the program who was living in a very dysfunctional family situation. Over the course of two years I was able to help this young man improve his grades and qualify for college. This experience reinforced in my mind the value of hard work.

139. Have you ever had the opportunity to serve as a mentor for a person aspiring to reach the same leadership level you are at? If so, please describe your feelings about this experience.

Answer:

Not having the opportunity to serve as a mentor does not mean the candidate will have failed to answer the question. If the candidate has served as a mentor to a peer, the interviewer will expect a description of the experience.

As an example:

There was a woman in my department that aspired to work to move up into a management position. At first this situation caused me some unease since I did not want to jeopardize my own position.

I did work with this person however, and she eventually found a position in another district that was in fact a better job than the one I was holding. I learned the rewards of helping another person to succeed.

140. How do you go about setting the example for the people who work for you?

Answer:

To answer this question correctly, the candidate should be able to provide a discussion of the characteristics she feels it is important for a leader to model in the workplace.

As an example:

There are many ways of setting the example at work. It is usually more effective for a leader demonstrate the character traits he expects to be followed, than to try and tell people how they should be acting in relationship to their job. As an example, a manager who is always 30 minutes late for work will have a hard time convincing other employer of the importance of coming to work on time.

141. How do you build rapport in your department?

Answer:

I manage a department with a workforce of 45 people and find myself spending several hours each month helping people to get along with each other. I am learning new approaches for building rapport and hope I will get to a point I don't have to commit so much time to building rapport.

As an example:

Some rapport building steps include listening, finding commonalities, treating people with equity and not jumping to conclusions when accusations are levelled against other employees.

142. In your previous or present job, how closely are you supervised?

Answer:

There are two answers to this question. The candidate may admit that she was closely supervised in her previous job, or she may say she had significant liberty in her present or previous jobs. In either case, the interviewer will be interested in how the candidate viewed and responded to the situation she was in.

As an example:

In my present job I have the liberty to complete my responsibilities as I see fit. I did not have someone directly controlling my actions throughout the day. I believe the liberty I enjoyed allowed me to be a much more creative leader. My department had the highest sales performance numbers in the entire company.

As an example:

The candidate may say that in his last job he had a supervisor controlling his every action throughout the day. Having someone looking over my shoulder can be very intimidating. I am always afraid I will make a mistake that will hurt my ability to keep my job.

143. What is the greatest number of employees you have supervised? How successful were you in this job?

Answer:

The greatest number of employees I have ever supervised is 60. This happened when I worked for a company working on private jets. I believe I was very successful. I think all the people working for me were very satisfied with me as their supervisor.

As an example:

During the period I just mentioned, I was responsible for work schedules, appointment schedules, training requirements and vacation scheduling. We always met our production requirements, and the people were happy with my ability to make sure everyone had time off when needed. I received a great deal of satisfaction during the time I had this job.

144. Please describe a management decision you were involved in that caused significant controversy throughout the organization or company.

Answer:

The most controversial decision that I was involved in surrounded the issue of health insurance benefits. Recent changes in the insurance industry have caused our premiums to increase by an average of 18 percent each year. Our management team made the decision to go with an insurance program that raised deductibles considerably.

As an example:

When I originally came to work for the company, annual health insurance deductibles for our employees were only $250.00. After we *had to make the change, our deductibles increased to $750.00. This caused considerable unhappiness throughout the company. After this controversy, the relationship soured between management and workers to the point that we lost many high-quality people.*

---

145. Please describe a time when you were called upon to lead your company's efforts to complete a public service project.

Answer:

This is an opportunity for the candidate to show enthusiasm for community service. The candidate may not have had an opportunity for volunteer work through their company and if they haven't, they should share something they did outside of work. If they did have the opportunity for community service through an employer, this is a good opportunity for the candidate to speak highly of the employer which always looks good during an interview, as well as share what role they played in the project and what creative ideas they contributed or how their hard work or efforts helped the project to be a success.

As an example:

I led our company initiative to supply teddy bears to children in the local cancer hospital. A large percentage of the people in the company donated money to purchase the teddy bears, and many people volunteered to go with me to the hospital and distribute the bears. Everyone involved received great joy at the smiles the teddy bears brought to the children, and the parents were incredibly happy with our company for doing so much for their children.

---

146. What types of investigative skills do you need to evaluate customer service complaints?

Answer:

The most important investigative skill is the ability to draw out the truth in any customer interaction. The second most important skill is the ability to stay calm under all conditions. Customers respond best when the person they are dealing with does not overreact to what is being said in the conversation.

As an example:

In a recent customer interaction, I had to determine if the company was truly responsible for the defective product the customer was complaining about. The customer was unhappy because the customer service agent did not immediately indicate the company would replace the defective product. I had to work my way through all the customer's arguments and determine if the company was responsible to fix the product.

147. Are there some general principles you have applied when seeking outside funding for an organization?

Answer:

The primary principle that I have always applied when seeking outside funding is to never allow the need for finances to drive us to violate our principles when accepting money.

As an example:

When I worked for an organization working for the wellbeing of homeless families, we were always looking for grants and other sources of money to fund our activities. I established guidelines that prohibited our funding department from seeking financial aid

*from any organization that did not fully support our efforts to get
homeless families off of the street. Often times we had companies try
and pledge us support who were only concerned with the publicity
they might receive from their contribution. We were not interested in
providing anyone with advertising.*

148. What is the best advice you can give to a person aspiring to a leadership position?

Answer:

The best advice I can give to anyone trying to become a leader
is to never abandon your values. Good leaders need to be
people of strong character.

As an example:

*It is important for future leaders to model good character traits
such as honesty, dependability and loyalty. If you model these
characteristics consistently, you will be well on your way to
becoming an outstanding leader.*

149. In what ways must the operation of a large company be the same as a small company?

Answer:

There are core values that are the same for large and small
companies. Core values that are essential should include
honesty, providing quality products and recruiting the best
possible employees.

As an example:

*Companies of all sizes should be honest with customers, employees,
investors and regulatory agencies. Business of all sizes should be*

providing products that give good value for their customer's dollars. Every business is looking for the most qualified workers they can find. After a business hires worker, it has the responsibility to treat each person with respect and with equity.

150. What part do you feel the ability to rapidly respond to changing market forces has on competitive advantage?

Answer:

Companies that are unable to react quickly to changing market forces will fall behind their competitors. If a company falls far behind its competitors, it may not be possible to regain any competitive advantage.

As an example:

One of my last employers' competitors failed to see the need to update the controls on their power tools to incorporate some of the latest developments in electronic engine controls. Our company's research found without argument that consumers desired these types of controls. Because the company I was working for was willing to rapidly change their products to meet consumer demands, we gained a very significant competitive advantage.

This page is intentionally left blank

7

Competency

Behavioral

Opinion

Situational

Credential Verification

Experience Verification

Strategic Thinking

Character and Ethics

Management Style

Communication

151. If you knew the person you worked for was making a bad decision, how would you handle the situation?

Answer:

This is a question designed to elicit from the candidate a response that indicates how she would handle a very disagreeable work situation. The candidates answer should indicate a significant level of maturity.

As an example:

The key to handling this kind of situation probably begins long before the problem arises. Everyone involved in management should be developing relationships that will enable them to have a respected voice in the decision-making processes of the company. The point is, if my boss is making an unwise decision, I should be able to come to him or her and respectfully voice my disagreement with what is about to happen.

152. As a leader, have you ever taken on a task that you knew you were unqualified to accomplish? If so, were you able to complete the task successfully?

Answer:

Since most people have been called upon to do a job that seemed to be beyond their ability, every candidate should be able to recount an occasion when they were asked to do something, they were not yet qualified to do.

As an example:

In my professional career, I had never managed a department of more than 10 people. When a regional manager over my department became seriously ill, I was called upon to fill in as the regional manager. The regional manager was responsible for 10 department

*managers, and a work force of over 100 people. I was scared to take
on the job, but with a lot of hard work, and a lot of help from the
other department managers, I was able to do the job and eventually
was promoted to the position.*

153. What steps do you employ to resolve conflicts in the workplace?

Answer:

There are several steps I take to resolve conflicts. The
seriousness of the conflict determines just how I will handle
the situation.

As an example:

*The first step is always to throttle down any harsh rhetoric, or to
move people apart and let emotions cool down a little bit. Secondly,
a conflict mediator must find a way to determine just exactly what
the facts are. No problem can be solved satisfactorily unless the
reasons for the dispute are discovered. Many people find themselves
in arguments and have no idea how the fight started. Thirdly, the
mediator must begin the process of building a consensus on how the
dispute can be solved. Everyone who is a party to the dispute may
have to give a little ground in order to find mutual agreement.*

154. What place do you feel listening skills have in your leadership style?

Answer:

Many people are not good listeners. I personally believe that
a good leader must be a good listener. Leaders must be able
to hear and understand the concerns of the people who work
under their direction and supervision.

As an example:

During the last quarterly management meeting, several of the department managers were trying to get me to understand a problem that had serious implications for the future of the company. I quickly came to the conclusion that I would not be able to work my way through the problem unless I listened very carefully to what each manger was trying to tell me.

155. Can you tell me of a time when you missed a critical deadline?

Answer:

To answer the question correctly, the candidate will be required to indicate whether or not he has missed a critical deadline on his job. If the deadline he missed is in the distant past, it may not be relevant to this job interview.

As an example:

About six months ago when I was working as a project manager for a large commercial construction company, I failed to realize that I had missed a very important deadline for ordering some essential construction supplies. The failure caused the company to miss out on a discount that would have saved thousands of dollars. My failure caused me to receive a reprimand from my supervisor. I will do my best never to make a mistake like that again.

156. Have you ever had to make a decision without having all of the pertinent information necessary to make an informed decision?

Answer:

Yes, there have been a couple of times in my career when I made decisions without all of the information, I needed to make a truly informed decision, and it did not work out to well.

As an example:

Two months ago, the company I was working for was experiencing a higher than normal number of customer complaints. On one particularly busy day the customer service department brought to my attention a customer complaint they were unable to solve through normal procedures. I was already busy with other work, and made a decision based on a hasty review of the case. I later found out the customer had provided incorrect information and the company sent the customer a voucher for a new lawn mower, when in fact the defective mower could have been repaired for a fraction of the cost. I now do my best to fully research every case before making hasty decisions.

157. Please explain your approach to solving complex problems.

Answer:

To answer this question correctly, the candidate must provide an approach to problem solving that is plausible. Just pulling something out of thin air will not satisfy the interviewer.

As an example:

I have learned that the very first step in solving complex problems is to move away from the idea of assigning blame for the issue.

Regardless of where to fault lays for the problem, the solution rests somewhere beyond the blame game. Next you need to step back and do your best to take an objective look at all of the issues surrounding the problem. No problem was ever solved without ascertaining all of the facts. A graphic organizer such as a flow chart can be very useful for determining the relationships between all of the facts related to the issue. By following these steps complex problems become manageable.

158. As a leader, what steps would you take to lead people to reach a consensus on a common goal?

Answer:

When you are working with people it does not take long for you to realize that everyone has their own opinion about how a job should be done. When an organization is trying to accomplish an important goal or reach an important milestone, the leadership must work with everyone concerned to build a jointly agreed upon consensus on how to reach the goal or milestone.

As an example:

The first step is to get all the concerned parties to sit down and systematically go through all of the pertinent ideas and find out which ideas have value, and which ideas are not relevant to the discussion. The team leader should start a flow chart so that each idea can be place in the proper perspective. If there are a large number of stakeholders in the discussion, the process of sorting through all of the ideas and coming to a consensus on the right path to take may take considerable time. The more people that have to be heard, the longer the process may take. It is easier to find common ground when the views of each party to the discussion are valued and allowed into the discussion.

159. Do you think it is possible to get people who do not like each other to work and reach a common goal?

Answer:

Yes, I do. If it were not possible there would be many organizations that would never accomplish anything important.

As an example:

The auto mechanics in the shop I oversee are a very independent lot of men and women. Many times, tempers flare in the shop because some of the mechanics guard their independence with a vengeance. The auto manufacturer of the cars our company sells recently declared a major recall of the fuel system on our popular SUV. In order to complete this recall on each vehicle, it required three different mechanics to coordinate their efforts to complete the job successfully. Through careful negotiation, and careful scheduling of each man's work, we have been able to return a safe vehicle to the customer.

160. What do you do when there are no regularly established procedures for the situation you are facing?

Answer:

When the company does not have an established set of procedures to go by for a particular situation, I make a decision based on what I believe would be in the best interest of the company. In some cases, I may have to subjugate the company's best interests to the best interests of the customer.

As an example:

Recently I was faced with a situation as shift manager when a customer was robbed in our parking lot. The customer had just purchased a shopping cart full of goods from our store and was loading the items into her car. The assailant ran up to her and took two of the most expensive electronic devises in her cart and ran off with them. We did not have a specific written procedure for meeting the customer's needs that day, so I decided the store would replace the items that were stolen at no cost to the customer. When briefed on the situation, upper level management agreed I had taken the correct action.

---

161. How do you determine which employees or team members to assign to jobs that require a high level of responsibility?

Answer:

The correct answer to this question should include a discussion of the candidate's view on the qualifications a worker should have that demonstrates responsibility. The answer should provide some justification of the candidate's viewpoint.

As an example:

There are three words I consider very important when I discuss responsibility; accountability, reliability and trustworthiness. These words describe the character traits I need to see in an employee before I will assign them to jobs requiring higher levels of responsibility. I want a worker who will stand-up and be accountable for his work, even if he has made a serious mistake. I need workers who can be counted to be on time every day unless providentially hindered, and I need people I can trust to protect the sensitive company information that is entrusted to them. When employees show me this level of responsibility, I can then assign them to more important jobs.

---

162. As a company leader, how would you respond to an accusation of child abuse by someone who reports directly to you?

Answer:

The law is very specific about the legal responsibilities for people who are in a position of trust. People working with children are required to report known or suspected child abuse to the proper legal authorities. Simply saying something to your boss is not sufficient, particularly if your boss does not take the required actions necessary to stop the abuse and report it to the authorities. Additionally, persons in a position of trust are responsible to take those actions that are within their power to protect children from continued abuse. If a subordinate reports a situation of child abuse, you must take the required actions immediately.

As an example:

The best example is a famous football coach who knew of child abuse, said something about it to his superiors, but no corrective action was every taken by anyone in the chain of command at that university. The coach should have gone to the authorities himself when he became aware that no one in authority over him was going to take the required actions to protect the children who were being abused by a university employee. There can be no tolerance for child abuse by persons of trust.

163. How do you ensure the decisions you make about operations in your department support the overall strategic goals of the company?

Answer:

The first place to start is to always stay focused on the strategic goals of the company. I use this approach to align everything I am doing on my job. If my decisions do not line up with or support the company's strategic goals, then I am moving in the wrong direction.

As an example:

I have a large poster in my office that boldly displays the company's strategic goals. When I am working by myself, or working with my management team, we strive to ensure that our decisions support those goals. For example, our company's primary strategic goal is to maintain a 25 percent market share of the global widget market. In order to reach that goal, we must maintain the highest quality product at the lowest possible price. If I decide to purchase raw materials at a price that is too high, my decision will not support the company's strategic goals.

164. According to your way of thinking, how important are the company's strategic goals to your day-to-day work-related tasks and operations?

Answer:

To be honest, it is easy to forget the company's strategic goals in the day-to-day drag of the job. However, when workers are allowed to forget company strategic goals, the work people are doing can get off track and take the company into areas it never intended to go.

As an example:

The company I am presently working for is very good at building retaining walls for commercial construction projects. The company strategic goals are focused on maintaining a considerable competitive advantage in this industry. Last year company leadership began getting involved in building retaining walls for homeowners. This trend caused us to fall behind our main competitor in the commercial construction industry. It took us a lot of hard work to refocus our efforts and regain our competitive advantage in our primary industry. I learned that all the work done by company employees must be focused on the established strategic goals.

165. How good are you at gathering all the necessary information needed to make a critical decision?

Answer:

I am very good at doing the necessary research required to gather all the critical information to make a decision.

As an example:

I have learned how to contact people and ask the questions necessary to get the information I need. I am a good researcher in the library, and I have developed outstanding internet skills. When working within a team, I have learned how to encourage people to bring forth the ideas and information they have that would help company leadership to make the right decision. In my last job, the people around me always expressed their confidence in my ability to get down to the truth of any issue.

166. Has there ever been a time you were able to predict a problem your company would face in the future, and you were able to present a plan that would mitigate the future problem?

Answer:

Forecasting has become a very valuable tool for businesses. I have become very skilled at examining historical data to predict future company performance. In many cases, I have been able to determine when the company was moving in the wrong direction and present a plan that would enable the company to maintain a high level of profitability.

As an example:

At a previous employer I was worked in the purchasing department. My job was to make sure that all the raw material we purchased was accounted for, and to ensure we were not paying too much for the supplies we were purchasing. In the course of my duties, I noticed our primary supplier was gradually raising prices without any prior notice to our company. The rising prices would eventually hurt our bottom line. I made a proposal to company leadership that we seek bids from a wide variety of suppliers. We did find a better price on the materials we were purchasing and were able to maintain an acceptable level of profitability.

167. How good are you at quickly solving problems that present you with large amounts of conflicting information?

Answer:

I am very good at solving complex problems. Regardless of how much information is presented in the original argument, I have developed the investigative skills necessary to dig down through all of the clutter and determine the truth of the matter.

As an example:

> *In a recent situation at work, I was presented with the job of getting a large construction project back on track. The project had become bogged down in a whole list of seemingly unrelated problems. I was given a three-day deadline to get the project moving in the right direction. I began by developing a graphic organizer that allowed me to put every piece of information in its proper relationship to the project's critical path. I met the deadline, and the entire project progressed smoothly through its completion date.*

168. As a call center supervisor, how do you control the different functions that are taking place throughout the center?

Answer:

Most call centers are very busy places. They have to be busy to justify their existence. I know there is really no such thing as a multi-tasker, but I have learned how to compartmentalize all the different challenges that are thrown at me throughout the day.

As an example:

> *In the last call center I worked in, I made it very clear to everyone in the call center that they just couldn't come to me and demand that I give them immediate attention unless it was a genuine emergency. If the problem that needed to be addressed was routine, the people in the center knew they could let me know they needed help on my e-mail. This system allows me to look at what needs to be done and set my priorities. Otherwise the stress of the job would kill me.*

169. How effective are you at meeting sales goals?

Answer:

I am very good at meeting the sales goals my managers have set for me. I make my living by making the sales goals that are set for me.

As an example:

In most of the sales jobs I have held, the senior sales manager sets the monthly sales goal for each salesperson. If you met the goal, there is generally a bonus awarded. I cannot imagine a situation when I would allow myself to fail meeting my sales goals.

170. How important do you think succession plans are for a company's leaders?

Answer:

I believe succession plans are an essential element of a company's efforts to maintain continuity over the long-term.

As an example:

As a company leader, I have always required my managers to maintain a succession file so their work could go on if they were no longer able to work for the company for some reason. Well-developed succession plans ensure that critical operations are able to continue regardless of what happens to any one person in the company. People come and go, but the company continues to produce a product year after year with little or no interruption.

171. Please tell me about anything you would have done differently in your career.

Answer:

If I had a chance to do something differently, I would go back and accept a leadership position I was reluctant to take when I was about 25 years old. I believe if I had taken the job, I would have been able to move up into a senior leadership position much sooner.

As an example:

As I said, when I was younger, I was offered a position as a district manager. I was not sure of my ability, so I passed up the opportunity. When I passed upon the opportunity, my boss became reluctant to offer me other opportunities that became available over the next two years. This situation slowed my professional growth and progression for many years.

172. Can you think of ways that social media can make you a better leader for your organization?

Answer:

Yes, I can; my interaction on Facebook for example, makes me much more accessible to customers and employees. I am able to discuss a wide range of issues as I reach the greatest number of people possible.

As an example:

There are a whole range of social media outlets that a business leader can be involved in. Each outlet has its own advantages, but the greatest advantage is the ability to communicate with people exactly when an event is happening. Take Skype for example, I can see the person I need to work with no matter how remote we are from each other. I think social media has made the company more profitable.

173. How important is the development of strategic goals to the future of a corporation?

Answer:

Every company should develop a set of strategic goals. Strategic goals provide a path that should lead to increased market share and to increased profitability. If the organization is not selling anything, strategic goals are still important. Non-profit organizations use strategic goals to ensure the organization does not stray from its mission.

As an example:

Let's say a business wants to become the leader in worldwide sales of cell phones. The company would then make a determination of what it needs to do to reach this goal. A strategic goal then might be that by the end of 2012, the company would have a 50 percent share of the cell phone market in Europe. Every operation of the company must be aligned so that everything the company does will lead to the accomplishment of this strategic goal.

174. How does a company develop a competitive advantage?

Answer:

Competitive advantage is created through the product value, product pricing, distinctive features or differentiation and quality of labor force.

As an example:

When a company is able to produce a product that is superior to its competitor's products in some way, the company has established a competitive advantage. Competitive advantage is confirmed when the buying public establishes the value of the product by new and continued purchases of the product.

175. What influence should a corporate leader have over corporate culture?

Answer:

In my opinion, corporate leaders are responsible to establish the corporate culture that will identify the company. If you want a company that offers outstanding customer service, then the emphasis on customer service needs to begin at the highest levels of the company.

As an example:

The Chief Executive Officer at the last major corporation I worked for decided to set the tone for our company in regard to our response to customer complaints and returns. The CEO established the policy that we would respond proactively to all customer complaints. Any employee who provided a negative response to a customer complaint would be in trouble. This is a corporate culture that puts customers first.

176. Do you believe close competitors for a specific market segment can co-exist peacefully?

Answer:

It may be a challenge to always maintain a level of civility, but I do believe it is possible for civilized Americans to co-exist even when working in direct competition with each other.

As an example:

A hardware store that I worked for previously had a direct competitor not too far across town. Both stores had the backing of major hardware chains, so we offered very similar if not the same products. Sometimes our employees really got into the competition, but there were many times both stores got together for meet a need in the community. Each company knew that free enterprise is what makes our economy work.

177. In your opinion, what affect should the creation of improved value in your product have on your company's competitive advantage?

Answer:

In my opinion, any company that can improve the real value of their products should be able to achieve a competitive advantage.

As an example:

Improved value may include a number of different things. Improved value may be lower prices; improved value may be that a company increases the size of the product it provides for the lower price, improved value may be the inclusion of new features, or improved value may include a longer warranty. All of these things may work to improve the competitive advantage of the company selling a product.

178. What are three key factors in achieving and maintaining competitive advantage?

Answer:

The three key factors that may experts agree are essential to achieving and maintaining competitive advantage are maintaining a leadership position in pricing, maintain a leadership position in the benefit provided by the product and maintaining a focus on keeping their product in a leadership position.

As an example:

Companies that desire to maintain the greatest possible competitive advantage will keep their prices at levels acceptable to consumers, will ensure the product they are offering provides the best possible benefit to consumers, and will focus the corporate culture on meeting all of these challenges. A company must work each and every day at the process of maintaining competitive advantage.

179. Please describe how consumer demand affects a company's efforts towards achieving competitive advantage.

Answer:

The single most important factor that tells a company they are meeting customer expectations is continued repeat sales. When people return to a business to purchase a product, you know that company has achieved a level of competitive advantage.

As an example:

The greatest example in the corporate world in Wal-Mart. Wal-Mart is one of the largest corporations in the country. People coming back time after time have provided this company with a tremendous competitive advantage over all other competitors.

180. How can a company use its strategic operations to support its competitive advantage?

Answer:

Strategic operations are those activities that directly support a company's strategic goals. Strategic goals represent the vision a company has for future achievements.

As an example:

When you think about what the terminology strategic operations means, you must consider all the operations a company goes through each day to produce a product. A strategic operation is a manufacturing process that makes the goods the company sells. Shipping can be considered a strategic operation that supports a company goal to get orders out within 24 hour of the time the order was made. If a company can get goods shipped within 24 hours, it may achieve a competitive advantage in customer service.

181. How does the effective leadership of management teams help a company maintain its competitive advantage?

Answer:

In today's emerging corporate structures, management teams have become ever more important. Many decisions that used to be made by senior corporate officers are not being made by management teams, making their work very important.

As an example:

I was recently on a management team tasked with the responsibility to find ways to update our company's labeling and packaging. We had been receiving regular feedback from customers that they were turning to our competitor's products because our labels were too confusing. After our team brought in design changes improving our labeling and packaging, many of our customers started purchasing our products again. It will take time to gain back our entire customer base and regain our competitive advantage.

182. How do you get corporate leaders to expand their strategic thinking, and embrace opportunities in the global marketplace?

Answer:

This is not so much of an issue as it used to be. Most of America's corporate leaders now understand that they must position their company to compete in the global marketplace. For the few who have their head in the sand, it may take their company suffering a significant reduction in market share to get their attention.

As an example:

There are a few companies in the United States that do not have a strategic global vision, but they will be gradually marginalized. The ultimate source of change must come from shareholders who see the return on their investment shrinking. Some of the old-line thinkers will gradually find less and less opportunity for employment in the 21st century.

183. How do you get company management to embrace change as a constant reality in the 21st century?

Answer:

Most people are probably resistant to change at one time or another in their life. Leaders must be convinced that embracing change will provide them with the greatest opportunity for the financial growth of their company.

As an example:

The experts tell us that 350 million people will move into the cities in China in the next 20 to 30 years. This migration of people signals great change in that nation and signals great economic opportunity. American corporate leaders need to embrace this changing marketplace and position their companies to sell the products the new Chinese middle class will need.

184. What methods should corporate leadership use to help employees embrace the company's strategic vision?

Answer:

Employees must be made to understand their part in the overall strategic vision of the company. It is possible for a person to come to work every day and do a good job and have very little understanding of what the company is trying to accomplish. Corporate leadership must use every available communication tool to get the message out to every worker in the company.

As an example:

Corporate leaders can use department meetings, emails, publications or face-to-face conversations to help employees to get a grasp on the company's strategic vision. A company will have a much greater chance of accomplishing its strategic vision if everyone in the company understands how important their work is in the effort to move the company forward.

This page is intentionally left blank

8

Competency

Behavioral

Opinion

Situational

Credential Verification

Experience Verification

Strategic Thinking

Character and Ethics

Management Style

Communication

185. What is the most important motivational factor in your life?

Answer:

To answer this question correctly, the candidate should be transparent about the motivational factors that have made her successful in her career.

As an example:

My family is the greatest motivational factor in my life. I have a wonderful family, and I am committed to providing the best possible life for them. In order to accomplish these things for my family, I need to be the very best I can possibly be in my chosen profession.

186. In your personal leadership experience, what types of decisions have been the most difficult for you to make?

Answer:

The answers to this question will vary widely. The interviewer is looking for an honest answer and is not necessarily concerned with a long drawn out story that provides little insight into the candidate's thought processes.

As an example:

The most difficult decisions I have been required to make are firing decisions. I have never been really comfortable when it came time to let a good employee go. It is not necessarily difficult to fire someone for cause, but when business realities force the company to lay off good people, I have a hard time dealing with the human issues that ensue.

187. As a leader, can you describe a time when you received significant criticism for a decision you made?

Answer:

To answer this question correctly, the candidate must discuss a time when a decision he made caused him to experience a significant level of criticism. The interviewer will not be satisfied with a discussion of an incident that caused the candidate to receive a superficial level of criticism.

As an example:

During a major construction project, I discovered that a mistake had been made causing the project to move in a direction that would cost the company thousands of dollars of unnecessary expense. I had to make some unpopular decisions in order to get the project back on the critical path. Many people were unhappy because the change of course caused some workers to have shortened work hours for a couple of weeks. I was able to get the project back on the path it needed to be one, but I was very unpopular for several months.

188. If I went to your present employer and asked the people you worked with why I should hire you for this position, what do you think they would tell me?

Answer:

This is question is seeking an answer that many candidates may not be very comfortable providing. The interviewer is looking for an answer that provides insight into the candidate's ability to articulate an understanding of how the people around them viewed their work. Basically, the interviewer wants to hear from the candidate why he should be hired.

As an example:

To the best of my understanding, the people around me would say that I am the very best sales manager in the company. I work very hard at meeting customer expectations, and I am always concerned about the wellbeing of the people who worked in my department.

189. Do you have a plan for achieving your personal and professional goals?

Answer:

To answer this question correctly, the candidate must be able to describe his plan for future professional growth.

As an example:

I have laid out a 5, 10- and 15-year plan for the goals I hope to achieve in my life. In five years, I trust I will be able to earn a promotion to regional manager. In 10 years, I trust I will have completed a master's degree, and in 15 years I trust I will be able to move up into a senior management position with the company.

190. How do your personal goals support your professional goals?

Answer:

My personal goals involve the things I can do for my family, and in that respect, my personal goals support my professional goals because I need to grow professionally to continue providing the things my family needs.

As an example:

I really desire to provide a much larger home for my family. I know my personal income will need to grow to $75,000 per year to be *able to purchase and support the home I want for my family. Yes, my personal goals do support my professional goals and desire for growth within the company.*

191. Are you usually successful at resolving workplace conflicts?

Answer:

My answer to this question is a qualified yes. If I am given time by the parties to a dispute to discover all the facts, and time to build a consensus, I can usually help people find a solution to a workplace conflict.

As an example:

I recently had to help solve a conflict between department managers. The arguments these two people were using did not seem rational. I was able to get these two men to calm down long enough to listen to what I was saying. In this case and many others, I was able to work through the arguments and find a solution that both sides could agree to.

192. Are you someone who maintains a strict schedule throughout the day, or are you someone who loses track of time throughout the day? Please explain your answer.

Answer:

The candidate can answer this question either way, just as long as sufficient explanation accompanies the answer.

As an example:

I realized a long time ago that if I did not maintain strict control of my daily schedule that I would not be able to get everything done that needed to be accomplished. I have an hourly planner on

*my smart phone which sends me alerts for each scheduled activity
throughout the day. So yes, I am someone who maintains a strict
schedule throughout the day.*

193. Are you able to maintain a positive attitude during a difficult discussion or during a dispute?

Answer:

Sometimes it is a real challenge to maintain a positive attitude
during a dispute. When people are making strong accusations,
tempers can become heated. I have developed an approach
that enables me to remain personally detached enough from
the emotions of the argument to be able to make rational
comments and decisions.

As an example:

*When a discussion over a dispute begins to heat up, I force myself to
keep my mouth closed and simply listen to the different arguments
that are being made by everyone involved. If you wait long enough,
everyone will run out of arguments, and then you can begin the
process of finding a positive solution to the problem. One the heated
comments have been made; you must not allow the discussion to
return to the negative heated comments that got things started.*

194. When you are leading a group of highly qualified people, do you ever feel intimidated?

Answer:

Yes, I have felt intimidated a couple of times in my career. It
is a real challenge to lead people who have more skills and
talents than you possess.

As an example:

I was tasked to lead a group of scientific researchers who were trying to find a way to mitigate the environmental consequences of an oil spill on sensitive wetlands. My job was to coordinate all the work this 20-person team was doing. I had to stay on my toes to try and keep abreast of all the scientific work. I know I was over my head on many occasions.

195. Is it possible for you to take negative criticism from your boss without having your feelings hurt?

Answer:

The answer to this question is sometimes yes and sometimes no. The main key is to make sure none of your negative emotions surface in a manner that creates a confrontational issue.

As an example:

Two months ago, my boss made what I believe were some very unfair comments about a decision I made for my department. I think jealousy was the basis for the comments. I realized I could not let my anger to cause me to say something that would cost me my job. This is an issue of a person learning self-control.

196. Have you ever publicly disagreed with one of your supervisors? If so, what did you do to resolve the situation?

Answer:

The candidate can take two approaches when answering this question. If the person has never publicly disagreed with a supervisor, then that is an indication of the person's loyalty to her supervisors. If the person indicates he has openly disagreed with supervisors, the explanation must be sufficient to convince the interviewer that the problem will not happen again.

As an example:

I have made it my policy never to openly talk about the decisions of my supervisors in a negative manner. I never talk behind my supervisor's back, and I do not listen to others who are trying to stir up trouble. If I have a complaint, I take it to my supervisor alone.

197. Are you more of a people person, or more of a technical person?

Answer:

The candidate has two choices. In either case, the candidate will be required by the interviewer to defend their answer.

As an example:

Personally, I feel like I have a need to be around people all the time. I like to surround myself with talented people. I believe that if I surround myself with talented and loyal people, I will be successful at any enterprise I undertake.

198. What do the terms governance and accountability mean to you?

Answer:

The word governance carries the idea of having the power to define the standards that people are expected to follow, and then having the authority and power to require people meet those standards. The word accountability carries the idea of a person's willingness to assume responsibility for commitments in their private life, and commitments to their employer.

As an example:

An employer has the power to govern his company through his authority as the owner or through his authority as the senior elected official of a corporation. The owner sets the expected standards of job performance and behavior for all of the employees. This is governance in the business setting. Employees and owners are accountable to each other in many ways. Employees are responsible to fulfill the responsibility to be at work on time each day and are responsible to complete day's work to the best of their ability. Employers are responsible to pay their employees a fair wage, provide the benefits they promised and are responsible to provide a safe and healthful work environment.

199. What was your response to a situation when a mistake you made came to light that you had not told anyone about?

Answer:

The interviewer is looking for a candidate answer about a situation that actually happened. If the candidate has not been in this situation, then the question does not apply. For those who can answer this question honestly, the answer will provide the interviewer with good insight as to the candidate's ability to take responsibility for his actions.

As an example:

A recent event comes to mind in which I found myself in a very embarrassing situation. The whole thing started on a day when I had to fill in for a worker on the production line. The line was moving fast, and as a result, I got behind and damaged a very expensive sheet of material that was needed for the item we were producing that day. I got a new sheet of material so I could continue working and set the damaged sheet aside. I did not tell anyone about my mistake. The night clean-up crew found the damaged sheet and reported it to management. I found myself in a great deal of trouble and had to admit my mistake to the boss. I don't think I purposely hid my mistake, but I ended up paying for it out of my paycheck. It would have been much better if I had told my supervisor about the mistake when it was made.

200. As a company leader, how would you respond if someone who reports to you said they were the victim of sexual harassment or abuse?

Answer:

Every business in the United States is responsible to protect its employees from people who commit acts of sexual harassment or abuse. If I receive an accusation of sexual harassment or abuse from an employee, I am required by law to take immediate steps to stop the illegal actions of the abusive employee.

As an example:

A female employee came to me one morning and said there was a male employee who was making sexual comments about her and had begun brushing against her in the hallway. According to company protocol, we had to start by giving the man an official warning to stop his inappropriate actions. If he continued the harassment, he would jeopardize his job, and may face legal action. No employee should feel threatened while at work.

201. As a company leader, how would you respond if someone you have not direct control over came to you and said they were the victim of sexual harassment or abuse?

Answer:

The correct answer is that every company leader is responsible to take every report of sexual harassment very seriously. The candidate should indicate that she would help the employee report the harassment or abuse to the appropriate person in her own department. In fact, the company may have a department within human resources to handle harassment claims.

As an example:

A young woman from the shipping department came to me and said there was a man her department that was making inappropriate gestures toward her. The woman told me that she was afraid to report the abuse to her boss because said the two men were friends. I went with her to human resources and helped her follow the procedures to report the harassment. I felt it was my responsibility to help the young woman be able to work in a non-threatening work environment.

202. What would you do if you became aware that your company's leaders were ignoring claims by employees, they were being sexually harassed or abused?

Answer:

This question is asking the candidate to discuss a very difficult scenario. If the accusations referred to in this question are true, company leaders may well be guilty of a crime. Federal and state laws require public and private organizations to take action when sexual harassment is reported.

As an example:

> *In this scenario, the best course of action may be to take the report to the state office of workplace equality. I understand that reporting suspected harassment or abuse to a state agency my cost me my job, but I have a responsibility as a leader to protect those who are the victims of sexual harassment or abuse. In this case, my action may save a fellow employee from significant emotional harm.*

---

203. Are you a person who will always take the initiative?

Answer:

> Yes, I always look for things to do at work. If there is a job that needs to be done, I will jump right on it and find out what I need to do to get the work accomplished.

As an example:

> *As a result of the fast pace in the manufacturing plant I have been working in, there always seems to be extra job functions that get forgotten or pushed aside for a variety of reason. These extra jobs are still important, so when I am caught up on my duties as the section leader, I go around the area and make sure all the jobs that have been pushed aside get accomplished. This effort frees up workers to concentrate on essential production jobs that must be done to keep the line moving.*

---

204. Has there ever been a time when you were asked to violate your personal values to get a difficult task accomplished?

Answer:

> Yes, there have been times when employers and supervisors have expected me to look the other way when they did things that were unfair to the customer. The justification

that is always offered is that company profitability must be maintained at all cost, but I don't like cheating customers.

As an example:

In my present job, we had a warranty claim that would have been very costly for the company to fully honor. The customer had the right to demand more from the company than the owner was willing to provide. Since I refused to treat the customer unfairly, my supervisor took over the claim and provided the customer with an inferior replacement product. I am sure this whole issue will end up in court. This is why I am looking for an employer who is honest in their dealings with customers.

205. What would you do if you knew that a fellow employee was stealing from the company?

Answer:

To answer this question correctly the candidate should indicate that he would report the thefts to the appropriate authority within the company. It is the company's responsibility as whether or not to proceed with any disciplinary action or criminal prosecution.

As an example:

When I was manager of a large jewelry department at a previous employer, we were required to take daily inventory of all the items we were supposed to have in stock. The inventory showed we were short of some jewelry items. I then had to begin observing the department more closely so we could figure out where the items were going. Finally, a surveillance camera caught a clerk in the act of pocketing an expensive necklace. I then reported the evidence to the store manager, and she took the investigation from that point.

206. What would you do if you knew a member of the company's senior leadership was stealing from the company?

Answer:

When answering this question, candidates are required to make a serious judgment about how reporting stealing of senior leadership would impact their position within the organization. There are only two places theft at this level could be reported; you could report the theft to the owner of the company, or you could go directly to law enforcement. Either option is a serious step.

As an example:

The interviewer is looking for an answer that provides insight into the candidate's ethical feelings about theft from the company. The candidate should affirm that she would report theft by senior company leadership to the proper authority.

207. What would you do if a fellow manager asked you to break the rules so he wouldn't get in trouble for something he had done?

Answer:

When answering this question, the candidate will reveal his ability to take a stand for what is right in a business context. Managers at any level should not be covering for another manager's errors. The best policy when mistakes are made is an honest admission of the error.

As an example:

Earlier this year a manager from another department came to me and asked me to falsify an attendance record so it would show this man wasn't at work on a particular day. Of course, I wanted to know why I was being asked to cover this is person, and he told me he had broken an expensive part on that day, and the boss had not yet discovered the loss. If the boss looked at the attendance record, I falsified, he would think someone else was to blame for the loss. I refused to cooperate with the lie, and in fact, I reported the problem to the boss. This manager lost his job over the falsehood, and I lost a friend that day.

208. Has there been an occasion when your personal initiative caused the boss to tell you to slow down?

Answer:

To answer this question correctly, the candidate must reveal information on his willingness to take initiative in the workplace. In the situation described in this question, the interviewer is looking for the candidate to reveal an incident in which he was working so hard the boss asked him to slow down. The answer will reveal whether or not the candidate considers himself an excellent worker.

As an example:

I can remember one occasion when we had a pressing job to get done on an aircraft we were working on. I had stayed late three days in a row to get the job done by Friday. Finally, on Thursday, the boss told me to go home at the regular time. He thanked me for my hard work, but he wanted some of the other people in the shop to show a little initiative to get the job done on time. I know I made a very good impression on my supervisor.

209. Why did you choose to become a call center supervisor?

Answer:

I decided to be a call center supervisor because I really enjoy working with people.

As an example:

Call centers are places that conduct business between people. I like meeting the needs of customer, and I also like meeting the needs of the people who work for me. For me, a bad day is when I am unable to meet the needs of the people I have contact with that day. The greater pressure I am under, the happier I am.

210. When a salesperson is trying to make a sale, is it okay for the salesperson to stretch the truth in order to make the sale?

Answer:

I do not believe it is ever a good policy to say things about your product that are not true.

As an example:

In my last job we had a young salesperson who was struggling to make sales. Since our salespeople worked on commission, not making sales quickly becomes a serious issue. This person was stretching the truth about the benefits of our product, and as a result, was making some very unhappy customers. The sales manager was forced to let this salesperson go for failing to be honest with customers.

211. Are there any situations in business that you feel justifies telling a lie?

Answer:

There is never any justification for telling blatant lie. Some people feel that telling a "white lie" may be justified to protect another person, or to keep sensitive information from being exposed. The candidate should be careful to word their answer in a way where they get the point across that they don't believe in telling lies, however they are also not going to provide individuals with confidential information that they shouldn't be and they are versed in ways to properly answer sensitive questions without having to tell a "lie."

As an example:

For myself, I do not believe in telling lies. If I always tell the truth and act with complete transparency in my job, I will not be put into a negative situation I have to get myself out of later because I didn't just tell the truth in the first place. At the same time, I understand that there may be times where I am asked certain questions where if I knew the answer and it contained sensitive or confidential information I was not at the liberty to share, I could also be transparent with that and say that I was not permitted to share the information.

212. Why is it important for a leader to set the example for all the people who are following him?

Answer:

The most effective way a leader can encourage compliance with workplace standards is set the standard by their own workplace conduct. When people see the standards are important to the boss, they are usually more inclined to voluntarily follow the rules.

As an example:

When I was working for a company that provided IT services for Wall Street financial service companies, I was expected to follow a set of very strict dress standards. Sometimes our technicians would become a little slack in their compliance with the standards. Company leadership always made it a practice to dress appropriately when they came to work. Without saying a word, our leaders were able to keep everyone on the right track.

213. As a leader, what kind of issues keep you awake at night?

Answer:

The candidate may provide a very wide range of answers to this question. The interviewer will be expecting an honest answer that provides insight into issues the candidate finds difficult to handle.

As an example:

I have a real difficult time when I am forced to lay off people who have been loyal to the company. During a recent financial downturn, I had to lay off three employees who had worked for the company for the last 10 years. These three people had families, and I had a difficult time dealing with the situation. I know I need to face these issues with much more objectivity, but I did not sleep too well for the next few nights.

214. Do you consider yourself a workaholic? How do you maintain a proper balance between you work and your personal life?

Answer:

No, I am not a workaholic. I have learned to maintain a good balance between my work responsibilities and my responsibilities to my family. I do not allow myself to become so engrossed in my work that my life gets out of balance.

As an example:

I have always worked in fast paced and demanding offices. When you are in this type of situation, you have to let all of your supervisors know that you have a family and you are not prepared to work over 40 hours per week unless there is a very special reason for being asked to work overtime. I will not work for an employer who will not recognize the value of my personal time with my family. I am ready and willing to do extra hours to meet emergencies, but I have a very full life when I am away from my job.

215. Is the character trait of humility important for a leader?

Answer:

Yes, humility is a very important character trait for a leader.

As an example:

Although people look for leaders with charisma, they also look for leaders who can do great things without constantly trying to get glory for themselves. I knew a man who was a senior corporate leader who was able to accomplish great things for the company through his talents and abilities. However, this man knew that much of his success depended on the people in the company. This man was able to share the credit with the people who helped him move the company forward.

216. Are you a leader who regularly challenges the status quo?

Answer:

I have challenged the status quo a few times in my career, but I cannot say that I do it on a regular basis. I usually try and find solutions to problems within normal channels.

As an example:

The last time I challenged the status quo, I almost got myself into more trouble than I could handle. In this situation, I disagreed with a decision the senior manager had made about the firing of a long-time employee. I felt the employee was being blamed for something he had not done. I bucked the senior manager and saved the woman's job, but I placed my own job in jeopardy. One month later, the senior manager found the person who was really at fault for the problem, and I was vindicated. I do not do things like this very often anymore.

217. What part do you feel passion plays in the ability to lead people?

Answer:

Passion is very important to leaders. Leaders must believe in the organization they are working for. A passionate leader will be able to help other people catch the vision of what the organization is trying to accomplish.

As an example:

My last employer was a non-profit organization that provided services for unwed mothers. Some of the cases we dealt with were very discouraging. Our clients were from low income families, so they faced many serious financial pressures. The director of the organization was very passionate about our mission and did her very best to help everyone in the organization remained focused on helping our clients make a new start in life. Our director's passion is what made the organization so successful.

218. How well do you receive feedback from the people you report to?

Answer:

I believe I receive positive or negative feedback from my superiors with a good attitude. I am always receptive to making the changes my superiors feel are necessary to improve my work performance.

As an example:

In my last annual performance review, my manager noted that I had been slipping my sales numbers. I think the problem stemmed from my slow recovery from the death of my grandfather. I need to put that whole situation in the proper perspective and get back to doing the quality work I know I am capable of doing.

219. In today's challenging corporate environment, how important are the values of integrity and ethics to corporate leaders?

Answer:

The values of integrity and ethical behavior are not an option anymore. There are many people in government and in the public realm that are watching the actions of corporate leaders.

As an example:

Many large corporations are still giving executive very generous performance bonuses each year. Many people in the public realm feel these bonuses are very egregious considering the difficult time average Americans are having making a living. People are watching to make sure corporate leaders are displaying ethical behaviors and are handling shareholder's money in an honest and transparent manner.

9

Competency

Behavioral

Opinion

Situational

Credential Verification

Experience Verification

Strategic Thinking

Character and Ethics

Management Style

Communication

220. Please tell me about a situation that caused you to discipline someone who was working for you.

Answer:

To answer this question correctly, the candidate will need to describe an actual situation when he or she had to take on the responsibility disciplining a worker who failed to correctly fulfill his work responsibilities.

As an example:

In a recent incident at my previous employer, there was a person in my department that was helping himself to lunchmeat products in the back-storage room. My first step was to give the man a formal written reprimand and inform him that his job was in jeopardy. The man was very emotional, but I had to work through the pertinent information to see if there was a way to get this man back on the right tract.

221. How do you deal with workers who are habitually late for work?

Answer:

The first thing to establish is that being habitually late for work is not acceptable. Employers who allow employees to arrive late for workday after day risk a significant reduction in productivity.

As an example:

From my perspective, I only give one warning for unexcused tardiness. After that I begin the formal discipline process which will lead to termination of the employee. The disciplinary process includes verbal and written warnings that are documented in the employee's personnel jacket.

222. How do you deal with workers who habitually fail to show up for work as scheduled?

Answer:

People need to be at work for the hours they are scheduled to be there. Employees can't decide for themselves which hours they will work. Failure to be on time when you are scheduled will bring you into the company's disciplinary process.

As an example:

I had to deal with an employee who refused to be at work when she was scheduled. I started with an initial warning, and then I had to bring her into the company disciplinary process. The company has a detailed plan of verbal and written warnings that are all documented on the person's personnel file.

223. How would you discipline a worker who insists on using inappropriate language around customers and even coworkers?

Answer:

The use of inappropriate language is unacceptable at any time on the job. The first response to the use of inappropriate language may be as simple as a polite request to be more careful in the future. If an employee refuses to be cooperative, then official disciplinary action will need to be taken.

As an example:

Your first response to employees who use inappropriate language should not be anger. Many times, a polite reminder will do the trick. Most organizations have protocols for taking disciplinary action on employees who refuse to follow the standards. Company leadership must set the example for the type of behavior that is expected on the job.

224. How would you deal with a worker who refuses to wear his work uniform correctly?

Answer:

Uniforms help customers identify the people in a store that can assist them with their shopping needs. In other cases, uniforms are designed to keep employees safe. Managers have every right to insist that employees wear their uniform correctly.

As an example:

When I was a shift manager in a local fast food restaurant, I had a young man who refused to wear his shirt properly. I was kind enough to warn him a few times that he was required to wear his uniform in a certain manner. When that didn't work, I had to begin the process of issuing official warnings. Sadly to say, this young man eventually lost his job over this issue.

225. How would you deal with a worker who refuses to use required safety clothing and safety equipment?

Answer:

This is a situation which cannot be tolerated. Safety equipment must be worn when required. If the employee refuses, he or she will be released that very day.

As an example:

I had a subordinate who was working in a shop environment that required the use of eye protection. The employee received the proper safety training, was issued good fitting eye protection, but refused to put his safety glasses on when working in the shop. We had no choice but to fire the man.

226. Without revealing any personal information, please tell me about the person you consider the worst employee you ever supervised.

Answer:

I had a young man working for me once that had no clue on how an employee should respond to the instructions he is given. This young man was habitually late for work, unproductive and always saying things that created dissension in the work center.

As an example:

This young man had the habit of going to an appointment in the morning, and never coming back into work for the rest of the day. Evidently no one had ever attempted to help this young man to reach even a minimal level of maturity. All the people in the shop tried to help him to no avail. He eventually got in trouble with the law and lost his job.

227. Without revealing any personal information, please tell me about the person you consider the best employee you ever supervised.

Answer:

I can remember a young person I had working for me that would never stop on his own. If something needed to be accomplished after hours, this young man was the one who would step up and get the job done without being told.

As an example:

One day we had a difficult job that had to be accomplished on an aircraft in order to get the plane ready to fly as scheduled. This young man stepped in and said he would stay after work and stay until the job was finished. The aircraft was able to fly on schedule because of the work of this person. If every person who worked for me was this conscientious, may work would not be hard at all.

---

228. What do you feel is the best relationship that a leader can have with the people who work for him?

Answer:

It is always best to maintain a professional relationship at work. It is okay to be friendly, but a proper working relationship must be maintained at all times. When things get out of order, it is very easy for the leader's authority to be compromised.

As an example:

The relationship between workers and supervisors must be kept at a professional level at all times. I do not allow people to wander freely in and out of my office whenever they want to. I do not allow myself to get involved in the office gossip, and I ensure my own conduct is above reproach at all times.

---

229. As a person working in leadership positions, have you developed a personal leadership philosophy? If so, please explain.

Answer:

To answer this question correctly, the candidate must be able to articulate a clear philosophy of leadership.

As an example:

A philosophy of leadership will include words like integrity, honesty and leadership by example. Other words that should be considered are empathy, understanding the ramifications of your decisions, justice and equity. It is important not to forget the ideas of good communication and having a strong work ethic.

230. Have any of the people working under your direct supervision ever publicly disagreed with your decisions? If so, how did you handle the situation?

Answer:

Yes, I have had subordinates openly disagree with my decisions, but I have tried to deal with each case individually. I make it a point the respond to the offense privately and try to ensure the dignity of the offender is not violated.

As an example:

The most serious violation I can remember happened over a decision I made to reduce the lunch period to one half an hour when we were far behind on our work. The change was only temporary, but there was one person who could not or would not stop talking to everyone in the shop about the issue. I finally had to take the person aside and inform her that further talk would force me to take official action to solve the issue.

231. What do you feel is the greatest thing a manager can do to help the people working in his department?

Answer:

To answer this question correctly, the candidate should present information based on his or her personal experience working in a leadership position. The thoughts presented in this answer should reflect and honest evaluation of the things the candidate has done in his own work to help the people working for him.

As an example:

My personal experience has shown me the most helpful thing that I can do for the people working under my leadership is to ensure they are treated correctly by the company. If I learn of any action the company takes that will not be good for any of my people, I need to step up and ensure the situation is corrected as quickly as possible.

232. Please tell me about a critical decision you made when your supervisor was absent. How did you supervisor respond to your decision when she returned?

Answer:

The question is looking for an answer based on an actual incident. Responses based upon imaginary situations are not satisfactory. If the candidate does not have an actual incident to talk about, he or she should say so and allow the interview to move on the next question.

As an example:

I can think of an occasion when the boss had to go out of town for a couple of days to meet with a client. I was left in charge, with instructions to call the boss if something came up that was too big for me to handle alone. While the boss was away, an important client contacted us with a serious complaint about a shipment he had received. I tried to call the boss's cell phone, but he was out of range, and did not answer. I solved the problem by sending a technician out on an expensive service call. When the boss came back, he was happy I took the initiative to keep an important customer happy.

233. As a person in a leadership position, how would you handle the situation if several valuable employees quit at the same time?

Answer:

My first thought would be that we had a serious problem affecting several employees. I would have to start from the premise there was something to fix on the company side of the issue. I was able to fix the problem, and the next step was to find out if the employees could be brought back into the company.

As an example:

Last January there were six employees in my department that quit their job all within a one-week period. These people were very important to our operations. I immediately sought out each person and asked them why they were leaving the company. The common thread through each case was the company was not promoting from within but was bringing in outside people for upper level management positions. After serious negotiations with company leadership, I received a commitment to change the promotion policies. Because of these efforts, I was able to bring three of the six people back into the company.

234. What is your personal approach to supervising employees?

Answer:

To answer this question correctly, the candidate will be required to express an approach to supervising employees that makes sense to the interviewer. The interviewer will be looking for an answer that indicates whether the candidate takes a strong leadership approach, or an approach that allows every member of the team to have a voice or some other approach that is viable. The interviewer may want the candidate to provide verifiable evidence of his approach from a previous job.

As an example:

My approach to supervising employees is very participative. I don't make decisions without talking to the people that will be affected. I don't have all the answers. Other people have valuable ideas to add to any discussion. There are a few times when I need to stand up and make a decision that may be unpopular, but this is the exception not the rule.

---

235. How would you help an employee who is having difficulty getting his work done successfully?

Answer:

The candidate should express a balanced approach to helping an employee having work related difficulties. A supervisor cannot carry an employee indefinitely. There is nothing wrong with providing some extra help, but there is a point when a decision must be made whether or not to keep the employee on the payroll.

As an example:

When I was leading the production department, I had a young man who was having a very difficult time getting the propane tank assembly installed in a timely basis as the RV rolled down the assembly line. I assigned an old hand to personally help this young man learn his job. It took an extra week of training for this worker to learn his job, but he turned out to be an excellent worker. The extra expense and effort were justified over the long term of this man's employment.

236. How effective are you at praising subordinates publicly?

Answer:

I sometimes get embarrassed when I praise people publicly, but I am working to improve my skills at telling people publicly how good of a job they are doing.

As an example:

At my previous employer I was assigned the task of presenting the quarterly awards at the quarterly department meeting. Some of the people who were given awards were people I considered my personal friends because of our close association at work. I had to learn to put personal relationships aside and provide the award the person had earned with a professional demeanor. The entire experience has made me a better manager.

237. What do you do to enhance the morale in your work center?

Answer:

I have several methods I employ to enhance morale. I start with the premise that each person in the work center has valuable things to say and contribute to the work we are doing. Secondly, I always find ways to provide positive feedback in any interaction with the people that work for me.

As an example:

In my present work center, I feel like we have a wonderful work environment. I make sure that I listen to everyone's ideas, and I make sure everyone has the opportunity for input before any decisions are finalized. If someone makes a mistake, I do not come into the room like a bull in a china closet. I always find ways to develop a positive outcome when correcting mistakes. I don't think there is anyone in the department who feels their job is threatened in any way.

238. What do you feel are good methods for bringing out the best in others?

Answer:

Good methods for bringing out the best in others include giving them an opportunity to share their ideas, giving every person in the company a fair opportunity to contribute to the completion of projects that are important to them and providing a fair wage for the work each person accomplishes.

As an example:

I have found that when a company values its people, it will create a working environment that brings out the best in people. We created this kind of environment at a newspaper I worked at a few years ago. The managing editor listened to everyone's ideas before he made any major decision. If there was a special project that needed to be completed, the editor found ways to get as many people as possible involved in the project.

239. How important should the issue of accountability be to corporate leaders?

Answer:

Accountability follows right in the footsteps of integrity and ethical behavior. Our society wants leaders at all levels to be accountable for the actions they are taking.

As an example:

If I made a mistake when I am dealing with a customer, I need to be up-front with the customer and with my supervisors and admit my error. Sometimes accountability has a cost to the person making the error. Accountability should make all of us strive to do a better job, and accountability should force us to display higher levels of integrity.

10

Competency

Behavioral

Opinion

Situational

Credential Verification

Experience Verification

Strategic Thinking

Character and Ethics

Management Style

Communication

240. Are you good at confronting problems with another person face-to-face?

Answer:

The candidate may answer this question one or two different ways. The candidate may indicate that he is very good at facing people directly when dealing with a problem, or he may indicate that he prefers to us an indirect approach to handling problems.

As an example:

If I have a difficult problem, I need to solve with another individual I try to take steps to lessen the impact of the upcoming confrontation before I go to meet the person. I like to send an e-mail ahead of the appointment to assure the person that I desire to solve the problem without creating unnecessary offense. This plan usually softens the emotional elements of the confrontation so I can look the other person in the eye and get down to the business of solving the problem.

241. Are you able to effectively discuss problems through e-mail or through texting?

Answer:

I believe e-mail and telephone texts are very good tools for discussing problems because the emotional impact of face-to-face confrontations is eliminated.

As an example:

Not only do I save time when I text a coworker about a problem, I reduce the possibility the coworker will be able to read something into my facial expressions that she may deem offensive. In business it is essential to use every communication tool that modern technology has provided. Additionally, e-mail communication allows me to reach a much broader audience with a single key stroke.

242. Do you think problems can be effectively discussed during a telephone conversation?

Answer:

Telephone conversations can be a very effective communication tool. Cell phones allow me to conduct my business from any location in the country. I can deal with problems when I have the time, and when I can find a place for a private conversation.

As an example:

In my previous job, my cell phone was my constant companion. As a sales manager, there were always issues and problems for me to solve. The telephone allowed me to travel to all of my appointments, and still keep track of all the business going on in my office.

243. If you are unclear about a point in a discussion or dispute, how do you clear up the misunderstanding?

Answer:

When I am unclear about a point in a discussion, I ask questions, and I listen carefully to the answers that are provided.

As an example:

During a recent management meeting, another department head made some inflammatory comments about some people who worked in my department. The initial accusations seemed to be a rambling recounting of unsubstantiated evidence. To get to the bottom of the issue, I began asking some very pointed questions. As the other department manager restated his comments, it soon became very clear that he really did not know what had happened to bring about the disagreement. It took me several days of asking questions and listening to the answers to find out what had really happened.

244. Do you consider yourself an effective communicator when conducting annual performance appraisals with subordinates?

Answer:

Sometimes I am an effective communicator, and sometimes I feel like I fall short in this area. I am working hard to develop better communication skills so that I can effectively communicate the information contained in performance appraisals.

As an example:

There was an incident when I was unable to connect sufficiently with a subordinate during a performance appraisal to get my point across. In order to get the correct information across, I had to ask another manager for help. This was very embarrassing for me. Since that time, I have been working to improve the connection between my written and oral communication.

245. As a company leader, how would you respond to an accusation of child abuse by someone you have no control over?

Answer:

Anytime a person becomes aware of child abuse in the workplace they are required to make a report to the proper legal authorities as quickly as possible. Anyone who hides their knowledge of abuse becomes complicit in the crime. Regardless of where you fit into the organization, you must report child abuse.

As an example:

I was the lead math instructor in a local community college when I received information that a teacher in the English department was taking advantage of his position to gain influence over some children who were coming to the campus for enrichment activities. After I asked a few questions, it became clear to me that the accusations had some basis in fact. I immediately talked to my supervisor, and to the head of the campus police. These authorities then took the immediate steps required by law to stop the abuse.

246. What is the primary way you communicate with your subordinates or team members?

Answer:

The primary method of communication that I have come to depend on is e-mail. Using the software provided by the company, I am able to communicate with everyone in my division very quickly. I can get the exact same message to each person, reducing the opportunity for misunderstanding.

As an example:

A recent change in Federal regulations concerning the sale of a popular drug had the potential for serious impact on our pharmacy operations. I needed to communicate the new regulatory procedures to everybody in the division that day. A letter would take too long, and I knew that I could not reach everyone through a teleconference. I included the information from the Federal government in the e-mail and kept our employees from making mistakes that would expose the company to serious legal threats.

247. Was there ever a time when you were required to coach a peer on his or her oral communication skills? What was the outcome of this coaching attempt?

Answer:

Yes, there was a particular time when the company hired a very skilled computer technician who had terrible oral communications skills. This man could fix any computer, but he was unable to stand up and describe to people what he had done.

As an example:

In order to help this man, gain the communications skills he needed to speak with senior leadership, I was given the job of helping him learn how to be a better public speaker. I soon found that all he needed to gain was some self confidence in his own ability to share his thoughts with other people. It took me about six months, but he began to come out of his shell and become a very good speaker.

248. How good are you at evaluating the non-verbal clues other people display when they are talking to you?

Answer:

The candidate may provide one of two answers to this question. The candidate can say she is good at evaluating non-verbal clues, or she may say she is not good at evaluating non-verbal clues.

As an example:

I think I am very good at evaluating the non-verbal clues that people display when they are speaking with me face-to-face. I can tell when they are mad, even though they are trying to hide it. I can tell when someone is hurting inside, and I can tell when someone thinks they

have something important to say, but don't know how to get it out.
My skill at reading non-verbal clues has helped me as a personnel
manager.

249. What steps do you take to clarify confusing instructions?

Answer:

The steps involved in clarifying confusing instructions include
asking questions, listening carefully to answers and asking for
written instructions if not previously provided.

As an example:

During the lead-up to a major project early last year, I received some
oral instructions that I did not understand. In order to gain clarity,
I sat down with my supervisor and asked several questions. When
it became clear to both of us that the problem was too complex to
depend on oral instructions, my supervisor directed the planning
department to prepare a written report that detailed very clearly
what each department's responsibilities would be in regards to the
project. My efforts helped everyone involved in the project to fully
understand what their responsibilities would be.

250. Have you ever had to deal with a situation in which you could tell the person on the other end of the line was a threat to himself or to someone else?

Answer:

Many people have never dealt with a customer of client who
is in a crisis situation. The most probable group of people who
regularly deal with crisis scenarios are emergency responders.
This question would be something that may be asked of
candidates applying for a job as an emergency dispatcher.

There may be some customer service representatives who have faced this type of phone call.

As an example:

About a year ago, when I was working as the night supervisor at the local emergency room, a man called who said he was going to commit suicide. I knew I had received some training in crisis intervention, but my skills were a little rusty. I was able to help the man calm down while a coworker found someone in the building who was fully qualified to help the man. I was a little shaky for some time after the call was over, but I learned there was a need for me to brush up on my crisis intervention skills.

Index

Leadership Interview Questions

Competency

017. Can you tell me the most important duties of a human resource manager?

018. As a fast food restaurant manager, how would you define or describe exceptional service in a fast food restaurant?

019. When a customer hits you with several unrelated questions at the same time, how do you sort through all of the questions and solve the issue that is the most important to the customer?

020. Which performance indicators do you use to measure the job performance of customer service representatives?

021. What are some formal or scientific methods for measuring customer satisfaction?

022. Please tell me what the steps are in organizing a sales team.

023. In what ways can rapid growth be harmful to an organization?

024. Do you understand the responsibilities required of senior corporate leadership under the Sarbanes-Oxley Act of 2002?

025. What is your definition of differentiation in the marketplace?

026. What is the relationship of differentiation to competitive advantage?

027. What benefit does a company's long-term competitive advantage provide to shareholders?

028. Please define a SWOT analysis.

029. How do you lead your organization or company to conduct a SWOT analysis?

Behavioral

030. If a group of people in your department were talking about you behind you back, what do you think they would be saying about you?

031. Please tell me what you believe are the two most important leadership traits a leader must have. Please explain your answer.

032. Has there ever been a time when you failed when working in a leadership role? Please explain what happened.

033. In what ways have you demonstrated leadership to the managers in your department or division?

034. In your career as a leader, which position brought you the least satisfaction?

Opinion

052. In your opinion, how important are values to the abilities of a leader?

053. In your opinion, how important are ethics to the ability to be a good leader?

054. In your opinion, how does a department manager display leadership skills?

055. Please tell me why you feel you are the best person for this position.

056. What attributes do you think are most important to a company's success?

057. How do you view the next five years of your professional growth?

058. How do you view the next 10 years of your professional growth?

059. Do you think the process of mentoring a person is an important element of that person's professional growth process?

060. Do you have an opinion of why leaders generally display the same type of leadership characteristics?

061. Please describe your feelings about consulting with team members before making decisions.

062. As simply as possible, would you please describe or define how you view the role of a leader?

063. Do you feel your leadership skills came to you through education and experience, or do you consider yourself a natural born leader?

064. What is your personal definition of the word cooperation?

065. Without revealing any personal information, please tell me about the person you enjoyed working for above all others.

066. Without revealing any personal information, please tell me about the person you considered the worst boss to work for.

067. How many employees do you personally feel comfortable supervising?

068. Would you please provide your personal definition of authority?

069. What are some responsibilities you have been assigned that were uncomfortable for you?

070. What are three things that contributed directly to your success?

071. What is your opinion of employee feedback programs?

072. Do you expect a leader to make the right decision every time?

073. Please tell me what you think of your public speaking skills.

074. How would you evaluate the place you are at in your career? Please use the following scale to make your evaluation; I am just beginning; I am a journeyman; or I am a mature expert.

075. If you had the opportunity, what kind of business would you start?

076. What is the most important factor to consider when hiring employees?

077. As a restaurant manager, how would you define or describe exceptional service in a formal restaurant setting?

078. What do you enjoy most about working with customers?

079. What is the most important lesson a call center manager needs to learn?

080. What are the most important skills a call center leader must possess?

081. How do you rate your own qualifications as a call center supervisor or team leader?

082. How important do you feel the issue of environmental sensitivity is to business today?

083. Is there anything about yourself that disappoints you?

084. What is there about you that makes you proud?

085. What is your favorite book on leadership?

086. How do you rate your ability to adapt your leadership style to changing conditions?

Situational

087. Please describe a situation when you needed to build support within your department for an idea you thought would greatly benefit your company.

088. During a period of difficult challenges, how did you keep the people working under your leadership motivated and working at the highest possible level?

089. If hired to work for this company, how can we best utilize your leadership skills?

090. Please describe your ideas about the need to reward team members for outstanding performance.

091. Do you have enough flexibility in your leadership style to adjust quickly to fast moving events or situations?

092. How effective are you at meeting critical deadlines?

093. Is there a major decision you made that you had to change after more facts came to light?

094. If you had to change a major decision at a later date because you realized you made a mistake, how did the people working for you respond to the change?

095. If you were a restaurant manager, and a guest found a hair or some other foreign object in his food, how would you respond?

096. How would you respond to a complaint from a very angry customer?

097. How do you respond when your subordinates come to you with personal problems?

098. How do you keep your supervisors from taking advantage of you?

099. Have you ever reported directly to the most senior levels of company leadership?

100. Was there ever a time you had strong competition for your job?

101. How have you supported the effort to build respect for other employee's opinions within the organization?

102. What would you do if you knew the company you were working for was regularly providing an inferior product to customers?

103. What have you done lately to improve the stability of the company you work for?

104. Please describe a time when you had to work with a diverse group of people.

105. Have there been situations when you have experienced difficulty working with a diverse group of people?

106. As a service manager, how would you define or describe exceptional service in an auto repair shop setting?

107. As a department store manager, how would you define or describe exceptional service in a department store setting?

108. As a college financial aid department manager, how would you define or describe exceptional service when provided by a college financial aid office?

109. Over the next few years, what do you feel are some of the most difficult challenges that people working in customer service are going to face?

110. How many customer interactions on average do you expect a customer service representative to deal with in a normal eight-hour shift?

111. Please tell me how you would handle customers who use inappropriate or abusive language on the phone, or face-to-face.

112. What will be the most significant issue call centers will need to address in the 21st century?

113. When you are directly selling to customers, how important is it to sell yourself, or sell the value of the company you represent?

114. How responsive should organizations be to the idea of social responsibility?

115. As you think back to your last employer, what differentiated your company from your competitors?

116. What part do company's employees play in setting a company apart from its competitors?

Credential Verification

117. Did you have any leadership roles while you were in college? If so, please describe your roles and how they helped you to develop your leadership style.

118. Please summarize the leadership experience you have that will best benefit this company.

119. Please describe your responsibilities at your last employer.

120. Throughout your career, have you always been an effective leader?

121. Since you consider yourself a talented leader, what has your present or previous employer offered you to keep you from leaving?

122. Have you ever had to deal with a situation in which a person working for you had an open disagreement with your supervisor?

123. If you are in a position that requires you to hire people, have the people you hired done well in their jobs.

124. What procedures or steps have you implemented at previous employers to improve productivity in your department or division?

125. How many years of supervisory experience do you have? Please tell me some of the job titles you have held as a supervisor.

126. At what point in your career did you realize your most enjoyable job would be found in a leadership position?

127. How effective are you at evaluating technical data? Please use the following scale as a basis for your answer: novice, semi-skilled, skilled or expert.

128. Please tell me which software applications you can operate proficiently.

129. As a customer service manager, what types of products or services have you worked with?

130. Can you describe some changes you have initiated that improve the way customer service representative communicate with customers?

Experience Verification

131. Please describe a time when you played a major leadership role in a special event.

132. Please describe a difficult project that required you to build consensus on a divisive issue.

133. Please describe a project or task that required you to develop agreement or cooperation between departments.

134. Please describe a time when you were called upon to demonstrate your leadership ability during an emergency situation.

135. Can you think of a time when your team was assigned the responsibility to complete a very difficult project? If so, how were you able to solicit a commitment from the team to work at their highest level until the project was fully completed?

136. In your career as a leader, which position provided you with the greatest satisfaction?

137. What are some ways a person in a leadership role can relieve the stress he experiences?

138. Have you ever had the opportunity to serve as a mentor for a young person? If you have served as a mentor for a young person, please describe your feelings about this experience.

139. Have you ever had the opportunity to serve as a mentor for a person aspiring to reach the same leadership level you are at? If so, please describe your feelings about this experience.

140. How do you go about setting the example for the people who work for you?

141. How do you build rapport in your department?

142. In your previous or present job, how closely are you supervised?

143. What is the greatest number of employees you have supervised? How successful were you in this job?

144. Please describe a management decision you were involved in that caused significant controversy throughout the organization or company.

145. Please describe a time when you were called upon to lead your company's efforts to complete a public service project.

146. What types of investigative skills do you need to evaluate customer service complaints?

147. Are there some general principles you have applied when seeking outside funding for an organization?

148. What is the best advice you can give to a person aspiring to a leadership position?

149. In what ways must the operation of a large company be the same as a small company?

150. What part do you feel the ability to rapidly respond to changing market forces has on competitive advantage?

Strategic Thinking

151. If you knew the person you worked for was making a bad decision, how would you handle the situation?

152. As a leader, have you ever taken on a task that you knew you were unqualified to accomplish? If so, were you able to complete the task successfully?

153. What steps do you employ to resolve conflicts in the workplace?

154. What place do you feel listening skills have in your leadership style?

155. Can you tell me of a time when you missed a critical deadline?

156. Have you ever had to make a decision without having all of the pertinent information necessary to make an informed decision?

157. Please explain your approach to solving complex problems.

158. As a leader, what steps would you take to lead people to reach a consensus on a common goal?

159. Do you think it is possible to get people who do not like each other to work and reach a common goal?

160. What do you do when there are no regularly established procedures for the situation you are facing?

161. How do you determine which employees or team members to assign to jobs that require a high level of responsibility?

162. As a company leader, how would you respond to an accusation of child abuse by someone who reports directly to you?

163. How do you ensure the decisions you make about operations in your department support the overall strategic goals of the company?

164. According to your way of thinking, how important are the company's strategic goals to your day-to-day work-related tasks and operations?

165. How good are you at gathering all the necessary information needed to make a critical decision?

166. Has there ever been a time you were able to predict a problem your company would face in the future, and you were able to present a plan that would mitigate the future problem?

167. How good are you at quickly solving problems that present you with large amounts of conflicting information?

168. As a call center supervisor, how do you control the different functions that are taking place throughout the center?

169. How effective are you at meeting sales goals?

170. How important do you think succession plans are for a company's leaders?

171. Please tell me about anything you would have done differently in your career.

172. Can you think of ways that social media can make you a better leader for your organization?

173. How important is the development of strategic goals to the future of a corporation?

174. How does a company develop a competitive advantage?

175. What influence should a corporate leader have over corporate culture?

176. Do you believe close competitors for a specific market segment can co-exist peacefully?

177. In your opinion, what affect should the creation of improved value in your product have on your company's competitive advantage?

178. What are three key factors in achieving and maintaining competitive advantage?

179. Please describe how consumer demand affects a company's efforts towards achieving competitive advantage.

180. How can a company use its strategic operations to support its competitive advantage?

181. How does the effective leadership of management teams help a company maintain its competitive advantage?

182. How do you get corporate leaders to expand their strategic thinking, and embrace opportunities in the global marketplace?

183. How do you get company management to embrace change as a constant reality in the 21st century?

184. What methods should corporate leadership use to help employees embrace the company's strategic vision?

Character and Ethics

185. What is the most important motivational factor in your life?

186. In your personal leadership experience, what types of decisions have been the most difficult for you to make?

187. As a leader, can you describe a time when you received significant criticism for a decision you made?

188. If I went to your present employer and asked the people you worked with why I should hire you for this position, what do you think they would tell me?

189. Do you have a plan for achieving your personal and professional goals?

190. How do your personal goals support your professional goals?

191. Are you usually successful at resolving workplace conflicts?

192. Are you someone who maintains a strict schedule throughout the day, or are you someone who loses track of time throughout the day? Please explain your answer.

193. Are you able to maintain a positive attitude during a difficult discussion or during a dispute?

194. When you are leading a group of highly qualified people, do you ever feel intimidated?

195. Is it possible for you to take negative criticism from your boss without having your feelings hurt?

196. Have you ever publicly disagreed with one of your supervisors? If so, what did you do to resolve the situation?

197. Are you more of a people person, or more of a technical person?

198. What do the terms governance and accountability mean to you?

199. What was your response to a situation when a mistake you made came to light that you had not told anyone about?

200. As a company leader, how would you respond if someone who reports to you said they were the victim of sexual harassment or abuse?

201. As a company leader, how would you respond if someone you have not direct control over came to you and said they were the victim of sexual harassment or abuse?

202. What would you do if you became aware that your company's leaders were ignoring claims by employees, they were being sexually harassed or abused?

203. Are you a person who will always take the initiative?

204. Has there ever been a time when you were asked to violate your personal values to get a difficult task accomplished?

205. What would you do if you knew that a fellow employee was stealing from the company?

206. What would you do if you knew a member of the company's senior leadership was stealing from the company?

207. What would you do if a fellow manager asked you to break the rules so he wouldn't get in trouble for something he had done?

208. Has there been an occasion when your personal initiative caused the boss to tell you to slow down?

209. Why did you choose to become a call center supervisor?

210. When a salesperson is trying to make a sale, is it okay for the salesperson to stretch the truth in order to make the sale?

211. Are there any situations in business that you feel justifies telling a lie?

212. Why is it important for a leader to set the example for all the people who are following him?

213. As a leader, what kind of issues keep you awake at night?

214. Do you consider yourself a workaholic? How do you maintain a proper balance between you work and your personal life?

215. Is the character trait of humility important for a leader?

216. Are you a leader who regularly challenges the status quo?

217. What part do you feel passion plays in the ability to lead people?

218. How well do you receive feedback from the people you report to?

219. In today's challenging corporate environment, how important are the values of integrity and ethics to corporate leaders?

Management Style

220. Please tell me about a situation that caused you to discipline someone who was working for you.

221. How do you deal with workers who are habitually late for work?

222. How do you deal with workers who habitually fail to show up for work as scheduled?

223. How would you discipline a worker who insists on using inappropriate language around customers and even coworkers?

224. How would you deal with a worker who refuses to wear his work uniform correctly?

225. How would you deal with a worker who refuses to use required safety clothing and safety equipment?

226. Without revealing any personal information, please tell me about the person you consider the worst employee you ever supervised.

227. Without revealing any personal information, please tell me about the person you consider the best employee you ever supervised.

228. What do you feel is the best relationship that a leader can have with the people who work for him?

229. As a person working in leadership positions, have you developed a personal leadership philosophy? If so, please explain.

230. Have any of the people working under your direct supervision ever publicly disagreed with your decisions? If so, how did you handle the situation?

231. What do you feel is the greatest thing a manager can do to help the people working in his department?

232. Please tell me about a critical decision you made when your supervisor was absent. How did you supervisor respond to your decision when she returned?

233. As a person in a leadership position, how would you handle the situation if several valuable employees quit at the same time?

234. What is your personal approach to supervising employees?

235. How would you help an employee who is having difficulty getting his work done successfully?

236. How effective are you at praising subordinates publicly?

237. What do you do to enhance the morale in your work center?

238. What do you feel are good methods for bringing out the best in others?

239. How important should the issue of accountability be to corporate leaders?

Communication

240. Are you good at confronting problems with another person face-to-face?

241. Are you able to effectively discuss problems through e-mail or through texting?

242. Do you think problems can be effectively discussed during a telephone conversation?

243. If you are unclear about a point in a discussion or dispute, how do you clear up the misunderstanding?

244. Do you consider yourself an effective communicator when conducting annual performance appraisals with subordinates?

245. As a company leader, how would you respond to an accusation of child abuse by someone you have no control over?

246. What is the primary way you communicate with your subordinates or team members?

247. Was there ever a time when you were required to coach a peer on his or her oral communication skills? What was the outcome of this coaching attempt?

248. How good are you at evaluating the non-verbal clues other people display when they are talking to you?

249. What steps do you take to clarify confusing instructions?

250. Have you ever had to deal with a situation in which you could tell the person on the other end of the line was a threat to himself or to someone else?

Some of the following titles might also be handy:

1. NET Interview Questions You'll Most Likely Be Asked
2. Access VBA Programming Interview Questions You'll Most Likely Be Asked
3. Adobe ColdFusion Interview Questions You'll Most Likely Be Asked
4. Advanced C++ Interview Questions You'll Most Likely Be Asked
5. Advanced Excel Interview Questions You'll Most Likely Be Asked
6. Advanced JAVA Interview Questions You'll Most Likely Be Asked
7. Advanced SAS Interview Questions You'll Most Likely Be Asked
8. AJAX Interview Questions You'll Most Likely Be Asked
9. Algorithms Interview Questions You'll Most Likely Be Asked
10. Android Development Interview Questions You'll Most Likely Be Asked
11. Ant & Maven Interview Questions You'll Most Likely Be Asked
12. Apache Web Server Interview Questions You'll Most Likely Be Asked
13. Artificial Intelligence Interview Questions You'll Most Likely Be Asked
14. ASP.NET Interview Questions You'll Most Likely Be Asked
15. Automated Software Testing Interview Questions You'll Most Likely Be Asked
16. Base SAS Interview Questions You'll Most Likely Be Asked
17. BEA WebLogic Server Interview Questions You'll Most Likely Be Asked
18. C & C++ Interview Questions You'll Most Likely Be Asked
19. C# Interview Questions You'll Most Likely Be Asked
20. CCNA Interview Questions You'll Most Likely Be Asked
21. Cloud Computing Interview Questions You'll Most Likely Be Asked
22. Computer Architecture Interview Questions You'll Most Likely Be Asked
23. Computer Networks Interview Questions You'll Most Likely Be Asked
24. Core JAVA Interview Questions You'll Most Likely Be Asked
25. Data Structures & Algorithms Interview Questions You'll Most Likely Be Asked
26. EJB 3.0 Interview Questions You'll Most Likely Be Asked
27. Entity Framework Interview Questions You'll Most Likely Be Asked
28. Fedora & RHEL Interview Questions You'll Most Likely Be Asked
29. Hadoop BIG DATA Interview Questions You'll Most Likely Be Asked
30. Hibernate, Spring & Struts Interview Questions You'll Most Likely Be Asked
31. HR Interview Questions You'll Most Likely Be Asked
32. HTML, XHTML and CSS Interview Questions You'll Most Likely Be Asked
33. HTML5 Interview Questions You'll Most Likely Be Asked
34. IBM WebSphere Application Server Interview Questions You'll Most Likely Be Asked
35. iOS SDK Interview Questions You'll Most Likely Be Asked
36. Java / J2EE Design Patterns Interview Questions You'll Most Likely Be Asked
37. Java / J2EE Interview Questions You'll Most Likely Be Asked
38. JavaScript Interview Questions You'll Most Likely Be Asked
39. JavaServer Faces Interview Questions You'll Most Likely Be Asked
40. JDBC Interview Questions You'll Most Likely Be Asked
41. jQuery Interview Questions You'll Most Likely Be Asked
42. JSP-Servlet Interview Questions You'll Most Likely Be Asked
43. JUnit Interview Questions You'll Most Likely Be Asked
44. Leadership Interview Questions You'll Most Likely Be Asked
45. Linux Interview Questions You'll Most Likely Be Asked
46. Linux System Administrator Interview Questions You'll Most Likely Be Asked
47. Mac OS X Lion Interview Questions You'll Most Likely Be Asked
48. Mac OS X Snow Leopard Interview Questions You'll Most Likely Be Asked

49. Microsoft Access Interview Questions You'll Most Likely Be Asked
50. Microsoft Powerpoint Interview Questions You'll Most Likely Be Asked
51. Microsoft Word Interview Questions You'll Most Likely Be Asked
52. MySQL Interview Questions You'll Most Likely Be Asked
53. Networking Interview Questions You'll Most Likely Be Asked
54. OOPS Interview Questions You'll Most Likely Be Asked
55. Operating Systems Interview Questions You'll Most Likely Be Asked
56. Oracle Database Administration Interview Questions You'll Most Likely Be Asked
57. Oracle E-Business Suite Interview Questions You'll Most Likely Be Asked
58. ORACLE PL/SQL Interview Questions You'll Most Likely Be Asked
59. Perl Programming Interview Questions You'll Most Likely Be Asked
60. PHP Interview Questions You'll Most Likely Be Asked
61. Python Interview Questions You'll Most Likely Be Asked
62. RESTful JAVA Web Services Interview Questions You'll Most Likely Be Asked
63. SAP HANA Interview Questions You'll Most Likely Be Asked
64. SAS Programming Guidelines Interview Questions You'll Most Likely Be Asked
65. Selenium Testing Tools Interview Questions You'll Most Likely Be Asked
66. Silverlight Interview Questions You'll Most Likely Be Asked
67. Software Repositories Interview Questions You'll Most Likely Be Asked
68. Software Testing Interview Questions You'll Most Likely Be Asked
69. SQL Server Interview Questions You'll Most Likely Be Asked
70. Tomcat Interview Questions You'll Most Likely Be Asked
71. UML Interview Questions You'll Most Likely Be Asked
72. Unix Interview Questions You'll Most Likely Be Asked
73. UNIX Shell Programming Interview Questions You'll Most Likely Be Asked
74. Windows Server 2008 R2 Interview Questions You'll Most Likely Be Asked
75. XLXP, XSLT, XPATH, XFORMS & XQuery Interview Questions You'll Most Likely Be Asked
76. XML Interview Questions You'll Most Likely Be Asked

For complete list visit

www.vibrantpublishers.com

NOTES

Made in the USA
Las Vegas, NV
01 August 2021

27373300R00103